"WHAT ARE THE BUTCHERS FOR?"

AND OTHER SPLENDID
CRICKET QUOTATIONS

WISDEN

"WHAT ARE THE BUTCHERS FOR?"

AND OTHER SPLENDID CRICKET QUOTATIONS

WISDEN

EDITED BY

Lawrence Booth

First published in the UK in 2009 by
John Wisden & Co
An imprint of A & C Black Publishers Ltd
36 Soho Square, London W1D 3QY
www.wisden.com
www.acblack.com

ISBN 978 14081 1331 8

A CIP catalogue record for this book is available from the British Library.

Cover by © Kja-artists

This book is produced using paper that is made from wood grown
in managed, sustainable forests. It is natural, renewable and recyclable.
The logging and manufacturing processes conform to the
environmental regulations of the country of origin.

Typeset in Haarlemmer by seagulls.net, London, UK

Printed and bound in the UK by MPG Books

CONTENTS

ACKNOWLEDGEMENTS

If I could shake the hand of everyone quoted in these pages, I'd probably come away with enough quips to fill another volume. Thanks, though, must go to the cricket-writing brethren, who usually have a pretty good ear for the repeatable *bon mot*, and to the players, for talking when they'd rather be doing more or less anything else at the end of another long, hot day. (If the quotations that appear here bear only a fleeting resemblance to what you actually said, please forgive the indulgences of our trade.) Special thanks to my agent, Jim Gill; to my editors, Charlotte Atyeo and Lucy Beevor; and the whole team at A&C Black for letting me get on with this enjoyable project in my own good time.

When I told a friend I was putting together a book of cricket quotations he wanted to know whether I was including a) the rude one about Eddo Brandes, Glenn McGrath and the biscuits, or b) the hoary one in which Viv Richards whacks a mouthy fast bowler (don't ask me who: his identity always seems to change) out of the ground and then tells him that, since he knows what the ball looks like, he can now go and fetch it. When I told my friend I was leaving both out, he looked relieved, before adding: "I might actually buy it now."

Any compiler of sporting quotations faces a dilemma. Indulge the reader with the comfort food of old favourites, or tease the taste buds by disregarding the set menu. I've erred towards the latter while not completely ignoring the former, because, well, some old favourites are old favourites for a reason. I don't know about you, but I still chuckle at the thought of Merv Hughes celebrating his dismissal of Javed Miandad, who had just called him a "fat bus conductor", with a raucous "tickets please!"

But a line had to be drawn somewhere, and guidance came from one of the genre's founding fathers. "Every quotation contributes something to the stability or enlargement of the language," wrote Samuel Johnson in his preface to *A Dictionary of the English Language* in 1755. On balance, "the bowler's Holding the batsman's Willey" didn't quite seem to make the grade. No, there wasn't even room for Holding and Willey in the Apocrypha chapter.

That's not to say there are not one or two Colemanballs in here – including one from the eponymous gaffemeister himself – but research threw up a lot more than the accident-prone. Acknowledgement should be paid at this point to my editor, Charlotte Atyeo, who suggested the lovely title and thus reminded me that some of the most memorable cricket quotations go beyond slip-ups and sledges: I defy you to read the exchange between those two great British institutions, Jim Swanton and the Queen, without a gentle smile.

If the butchers and their *raison d'être* stand for a whole sub-culture of possibilities (sorry, but I couldn't resist throwing in some observations from across the pond, beginning with Mike Marqusee's righteous and rightful indignation), then the adjective in the subtitle is applied in the loosest possible way.

"Splendid" has been stretched to its linguistic confines, but – roughly translated for the purposes of this book – it means any of the following: funny, farcical, rude, ribald, sad, stupid, eccentric, eclectic, pompous, preening, quizzical, quixotic, stereotypical, self-deprecating and a few other things that may occur to you as you begin browsing. Basically, it's a typically cricket-like synonym for "good".

Books of cricket quotations have been compiled before, of course, so I was keen to convey a sense of the game as it is in the new millennium. But I was drawn as far back as the 18th century, for there are too many gems to ignore from the days before cricket became the money-spinning, politically fraught, lightning-fast pastime it occasionally feels like today. I wasn't sure I'd find anything more deliciously self-important than James Pycroft's description in 1751 of cricket as "a standing panegyric on the English character". But you will probably agree a few claims in the pages ahead run him close.

Today's pronouncements are more likely to reflect the ethical dilemma – or otherwise – of accepting Perspex boxes of cash from Texan billionaires later accused of fraud; the rise and rise of India; and the increasing hold exerted by Twenty20, which has a chapter all to itself. There is even, with heavy heart, a nod to the terrifying events in Lahore in March, when not just the Sri Lankan team, match officials and Pakistani police came under attack but, it seemed, the entire game.

The book is arranged thematically and I hope you will indulge one or two of the more extreme flights of fancy. Cricket and Food may not be a topic you have spent much time thinking about – much less Cricket and

Animals – but you would be surprised what you find when you thumb through a library of cricket books. You might be just as surprised at the wealth of gems to be unearthed from the obituaries section of the more recent *Wisdens*. The small section on Cricket and Mortality is a respectful doff of the helmet in the direction of a yellow book bigger than this one.

Above all, I've been very lucky to have been asked to plunder cricket's astonishingly broad bibliography and then some. From WG to KP, George Gunn to Graham Gooch, Groucho Marx to, yes, Rafa Benitez, this absurd sport of ours just keeps on churning out the bons mots.

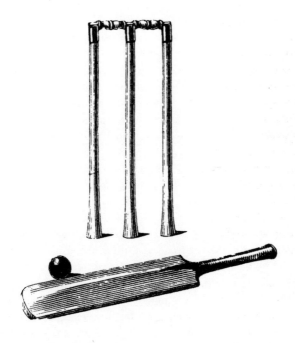

CHAPTER 1

TASTERS

"Life is an elaborate metaphor for cricket" – *American novelist* **Marvin Cohen**

"Cricket propagates a spirit of idleness at a juncture when, with the utmost industry, our debts, taxes and decay of trade will scarce allow us to get bread" – **The Gentleman's Magazine** *in 1743*

"The psychology of the game is accurately condensed in these few words 'It's not cricket'" – *Second-ever captain of the English cricket team* **Lord Harris**

"I tend to believe that cricket is the greatest thing that God ever created on earth … certainly greater than sex, although sex isn't too bad either" – *Playwright* **Harold Pinter**, *who years later would claim "that was a joke"*

"Personally I have always looked upon cricket as organised loafing" – **William Temple**, *Archbishop of Canterbury*

"Sometimes, when I feel a little exhausted with it all and the world's sitting heavily on my head, I pick up a *Wisden* and read about Len Hutton's 37 in 24 minutes in Sydney in 1946" – *Pinter again*

"Cricket civilises people and creates good gentlemen. I want everyone to play cricket in Zimbabwe; I want ours to be a nation of gentlemen" – *Robert Mugabe in 1984*

"Say that cricket has nothing to do with politics and you say that cricket has nothing to do with life" – *Journalist and cricket commentator* **John Arlott**

"There is a particular pleasure in listening to cricket in a country where it doesn't exist" – *Actor and writer* **Stephen Fry**

"Paradoxically, to be fun, cricket must be serious" – *Cricket journalist and commentator* **Christopher Martin-Jenkins**

"Golf is a game to be played between cricket and death" – *Hampshire captain* **Colin Ingleby-Mackenzie**

"If Stalin had learned to play cricket, the world might now be a better place" – **Richard Downey**, *Archbishop of Liverpool*

"Cricketer: a creature very nearly as stupid as a dog" – *Journalist and author* **Bernard Levin**

"I doubt if there be any scene in the world more animating or delightful than a cricket match" – *Novelist* **Mary Russell Mitford** *in* Our Village

"I certainly don't want to walk into an office too quickly because when the sun's out there's no better place to be than on the cricket field" – *Somerset and former England cricketer* **Marcus Trescothick**

"Cricket is a game full of forlorn hopes and sudden dramatic changes of fortune and its rules are so ill-defined that their interpretation is partly an ethical business" – *Author* **George Orwell**

"I am horrified that anyone should bring a knife when coming to watch cricket, unless it was for a delicious picnic" – *MCC president* **Colin Ingleby-Mackenzie** *reacts to news that a member of the club was being investigated by police for drawing a knife on another, who was using a mobile phone*

"A great advert for cricket" – *BBC football commentator* **Mark Lawrenson** *yawns after the first half of the 2007 FA Cup final between Manchester United and Chelsea*

"Years lost in early life are irrecoverable, particularly in cricket" – *Kent and England wicket-keeper* **Les Ames**

"A Test match is like a painting. A one-day match is like a Rolf Harris painting" – *Australia captain* **Ian Chappell**

"Cricket, a team game? Teams play, and one team is to be willed to victory. But it is the individual who remains in the memory, he who has purged the emotions by delight and fear" – *Novelist VS Naipaul*

"Cricket is the only game where you are playing against eleven of the other side and ten of your own" – *Mathematician GH Hardy*

"Mike, you're the only one who understands that it doesn't really matter" – *John Arlott to England captain Mike Brearley*

"There are 100,000 million stars in our galaxy and 1,000 million galaxies. Many a world must be inhabited. I am sure cricket must be being played elsewhere – they must be if they are civilised" – *Astronomer Patrick Moore*

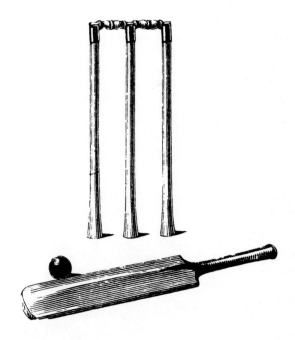

CHAPTER 2

THE ALTAR OF CRICKET

"Cricket is unalloyed by love of lucre and mean jealousies … the approbation and applause of the spectators being the sole reward" – *MCC president **Lord Frederick Beauclerk** in 1838. Beauclerk, who liked a gamble, wasn't immune to the love of lucre himself*

"The game of cricket, philosophically considered, is a standing panegyric on the English character: none but an orderly and sensible race of people would so amuse themselves" – *Author **James Pycroft** in 1851, waxing pompous in* The Cricket Field

"As artists go to Italy to do homage to the great Masters, as pilgrims go to Jerusalem to worship at a shrine, or as students in the Middle Ages went to the chief seats of learning in places where science and philosophy had made their home, so now the Parsees are going to England to do homage to the English cricketers" – *The Mayor of Bombay **Pherozeshah Mehta** provides the Parsees with an old-style pep-talk ahead of their tour of England in 1886*

"It is one of the greatest contributions which the British people have made to the cause of humanity" – *Indian-born England batsman **Kumar Shri Ranjitsinhji***

"There is no cricketer worthy of the name who would not be glad to sacrifice himself if he could to win the victory for his side" – *Bishop **Welldon** of Calcutta to a Japanese audience in 1906*

"It is an institution, a passion, one might say a religion. It has got into the blood of the nation, and wherever British men and women are gathered together there will the stumps be pitched" – *Lord **Harris** on the eve of the First World War*

"To play it keenly, honourably, generously, self-sacrificingly is a moral lesson in itself, and the class-room is God's air and sunshine" – *Lord Harris again, this time in a letter to* The Times *on his 80th birthday in 1931*

"There is no game which calls forth so many fine attributes, which makes so many demands on its votaries, and, that being so, all who love it as players, as officials or spectators must be careful lest anything they do should do it harm" – *Pelham Warner, England manager, at a press conference on the Bodyline tour in 1932-33*

"If I knew I was going to die today, I think I should still want to hear the cricket scores" – *Mathematician GH Hardy*

"We need more team-work, more patience and more unselfishness. To put the matter briefly we need more of the spirit of cricket" – *Somerset supporter and military man Major CHB Pridham, fearing the collapse of the Empire*

"In no other game does the law of averages get to work so potently, so mysteriously" – *Writer and critic Neville Cardus*

"Halfway between the Ten Commandments and Enid Blyton" – *Right-arm fast-medium bowler JJ Warr on the prose style of old-school doyen Jim Swanton*

"They've elected Swanton pope" – *Australian journalist Jack Fingleton spots white smoke billowing from a chimney near Lord's*

"Few things are more deeply rooted in the collective imagination of the English than the village cricket match. It stirs a romantic illusion about the rustic way of life, it suggests a tranquil and unchanging order in an age of bewildering flux, and it persuades a lot of townsfolk that that is where they would rather be" – *Author Geoffrey Moorhouse in* The Best Loved Game *taps into the rural-idyll theory of the game*

"Cricketers are brave men and, at the same time, so casual, so apparently unexcited; and when they are locked in a really vital struggle, and yet behave so coolly, they restore one's faith in human dignity; for to be valiant and calm is a marvellous human combination" – *Journalist Colin MacInnes in* New Society *in 1963*

"In other sports, people have no time to think; a cricket match is a storehouse of thought, of thought occasioned by the game itself, by the beauty, wit, or intelligence of one's companion, or simply a private unravelling of problems, personal, political, moral" – *Writer and journalist Alan Ross*

"Cricket seems to me to be richer in potential, deeper in its emotional and cerebral possibilities and wider in artistic scope than all games" – *Writer and cartoonist* **Bernard Hollowood** *in* Cricket on the Brain *in 1970*

"For people to whom cricket was a religion, we were heretics" – *Greg Chappell on his decision to join Kerry Packer's World Series Cricket*

"Like poets, cricketers spend unimaginable numbers of hours doing something as near pointless as possible, trying to dig an elusive perfection out of themselves in the face of an infinite number of variables, and as a result a large proportion of their lives belongs to the realm of the mystical" – *Novelist* **PJ Kavanagh** *in his essay 'The Mystery of Cricket'*

"Fifty years from now, Britain will still be the country of long shadows on county grounds, warm beer, invincible green suburbs, dog lovers and pool fillers and – as George Orwell said – 'old maids cycling to Holy Communion through the morning mist'" – *Former prime minister* **John Major** *in 1993*

"I have to wonder whether man is too weak to run a game like cricket. Maybe cricket is a perfect game in a sort of platonic sense, the paradigm of cricket" – *Actor and writer* **Stephen Fry** *in a speech to the MCC in 2007*

"It is so freakish in its ability to reinvent itself, to grow with the times, to spread itself around the globe and not lose the heart of its mystery, which is that strange blend of the tactical, the intellectual, the aesthetic and the athletic" – *Fry again*

"There is a widely held and quite erroneous belief that cricket is just another game" – **Prince Philip**

CRICKET AND GOD

"It's like bowling to God on concrete" – *RC Robertson-Glasgow after labouring for Somerset against Surrey's Jack Hobbs and Andy Sandham at The Oval*

"My dear Warner, anything that tends to the prestige of England is worth praying for" – *Bishop Welldon responds to Pelham Warner's question about whether it is wrong to pray to beat Australia*

"I said my prayers regularly and I remember after 'Gentle Jesus…' and 'God bless…' I always added 'Please God let me play cricket for Sussex regularly.' I added the 'regularly' because I thought the Almighty might fob me off with an odd game against Oxford or Cambridge" – *George Cox in* The Cricketer *in 1981*

"God bless Hobbs, God bless Hayward, God bless Hayes, God bless Hitch and God bless leg-byes" – *Unnamed Surrey supporter hedges his bets, as told by Cox*

"Here is a piece of what I should regard as direct service to the wider interests of the Kingdom of God. And as I understand it there really is a crying need for someone to bring back into the higher ranks of English cricket a sort of moral decisiveness which has been slipping" – *Archbishop of Canterbury Geoffrey Fisher persuades David Sheppard to defer ordination and instead captain England*

"It isn't fair. Look who you've got on your side" – *Australia captain Ian Johnson spots Sheppard on the England balcony before the Old Trafford Test of 1956. Jim Laker takes 19 wickets and Australia lose by an innings*

"Matthew Hayden copped some flak this week when a commentator questioned why the devout Christian crossed himself only after scoring a century for Australia and not for Queensland. That's easily explained – no one watches state cricket, not even God" – *Journalist Doug Conway in the* Canberra Times

CRICKET AND GOD

"Allah was with me today" – *Pakistan's **Javed Miandad** to England's Derek Pringle after Pringle had a convincing shout for lbw turned down in the 1992 World Cup final before Javed had scored*

"I knew that God was on our side" – *Pakistan captain **Imran Khan** confirms as much after the aforementioned match*

"I am a Buddhist and I think we have done some merit in our previous birth to escape with minor injuries" – *Sri Lanka captain **Mahela Jayawardene** after escaping unscathed from the terrorist attack in Lahore in March 2009*

CHAPTER 3

AROUND THE WORLD IN NINE NATIONS

AUSTRALIA

"The mystery of cricket is not that Australians play it well, but that they play it at all. It has always seemed to me a game too much restrained for their rough-and-tumble Australian temperament" – *American author Bill Bryson*

"If people look for a definition of cricket in Australia, they will say Don Bradman. That will be the case for the next 400 to 500 years" – *One famous captain, Steve Waugh, on another*

"It's nice to have beaten Bradman at something" – *Ted Martin, a Western Australia leg-spinner, becomes the first Australian first-class cricketer to live to 100. Bradman died at the age of 92; Martin departed on 101*

"On a rest day during the Indian tour in 1977-78, Don Bradman was around in the nets. I was bowling only leg-spin to him, but he had a couple of young blokes trying to get him out. With no pads, no nothing. For a 69 year old, he belted the hell out of them on a turf wicket. And he hadn't batted for 20 years. I went back in and said, 'Why isn't this bastard playing with us tomorrow?' That's how good I thought he was" – *Fast bowler Jeff Thomson is convinced that the past is another country*

"I thought, 'Stuff that stiff upper lip crap. Let's see how stiff it is when it's split" – *Thomson again, this time with his view of the average Englishman*

"[Dennis] Lillee and Thomson remain a combination to conjure with, as sinister in England as Burke and Hare, or Bismarck and Tirpitz" – *Writer and historian Gideon Haigh on Australia's fearsome new-ball attack of the 1970s*

"Blimey, he's just knocked St George off his 'orse" – *England seamer* **Geoff Arnold** *at Sydney in 1974-75 after Keith Fletcher is hit on the head by a rampant Lillee*

"Bloody hell, who have we got here, Groucho Marx?" – *Jeff Thomson greets David Steele, the grey-haired, bespectacled England batsman on Test debut at Lord's in 1975*

"Australia is an amazing country to tour. Beautiful, dazzling and seductive, it can also be like the female spider that kills and eats her unsuspecting mate shortly after the most amazing copulation" – *South African journalist* **Neil Manthorp** *ahead of his country's trip Down Under in 2008-09. South Africa resisted temptation to win the Test series 2-1*

"Len Hutton always said to win in Australia you have to be 25 per cent better than they are, firstly because the conditions are foreign to you, and secondly you have to overcome disadvantages like the heat and sometimes rather ordinary umpiring" – *England fast bowler* **Frank Tyson** *does little to dispel the stereotype of the whingeing Pom*

"I admire the Australians' approach to the game; they have the utmost ability for producing that little extra, or instilling into the opposition an inferiority complex that can have, and has had, a crushing effect" – *England captain* **Len Hutton**

"We find it both amusing and amazing how they always talk it up with about 12 months to go, telling everyone that they've finally got the team to beat us" – *Seam bowler* **Glenn McGrath**, *on England's habitual confidence ahead of an Ashes series, proves Hutton's point*

"It's hard to imagine an Australian player doing it" – *So does* **Ricky Ponting**, *after Brian Lara puts his unbeaten quadruple-century ahead of West Indies' chances of beating England in Antigua in 2004*

"We all admired and liked the Australians of those days. But, by Jove, we did like beating them!" – *Golden Age England all-rounder* **CB Fry**

"I have on occasions taken a quite reasonable dislike to the Australians"
– *England batsman and future chairman of selectors* **Ted Dexter**

"Australians have no inhibitions" – *Len Hutton*

"The Australian plays cricket to win: he has usually left it to Mr Warner
to make Empire-binding speeches" – **Neville Cardus**, *cricket correspondent of
the* Manchester Guardian, *on Australia and the England manager Pelham Warner*

"We've won it a few times so, yeah, we'd like to see what it looks like" –
Steve Waugh, *speaking ahead of the 2002-03 Ashes, on the urn, kept in a glass case at
Lord's no matter what*

"When appealing the Australians make a statement; we ask a question"
– *England and Somerset off-spinner* **Vic Marks**

"He's a smashing lad – very un-Australian" – *Sussex captain* **Chris Adams** *on
Ryan Harris, who played one game for the county in 2008 before returning to
Queensland…*

"We've said for the last couple of years that we want to be known as good
people and not just good players" – *…the kind of comment which provoked this
piece of introspection from* **Ricky Ponting**

"It's an oxymoron to say there's a weak Australian side – there's no such
thing" – *New Zealand captain* **Stephen Fleming**

"Take a deep breath and play somebody else" – *Fleming on the best way of
tackling Australia*

"I haven't got a blue blazer and I don't have dandruff" – *Renegade opening
batsman* **David Hookes** *on why he was never a cricket administrator*

"Enough to make you puke" – *England captain* **Mike Atherton** *on Steve
Waugh's decision to wear his baggy green – the official Australian Cap – while
watching Pat Rafter play tennis at Wimbledon*

"It is a $5 bit of cloth. I haven't got one, haven't had one since the day I finished. I don't need to look at an Australian cap to remind me of what I did" – *Former captain turned outspoken commentator* **Ian Chappell** *on the baggy green*

"Because my mates have retired" – **Rod Marsh** *on why he decided to quit at the same time as Dennis Lillee and Greg Chappell in 1983-84*

"I noticed them at the start of last summer using the England players' nicknames in the press and I thought 'We're in a bit of trouble here'" – **Steve Waugh** *presages Australia's 2005 Ashes defeat*

"Ian Botham would make a great Aussie" – *Jeff Thomson*

"We're a nation of sports nuts and piss-takers and all I've done is combine the two" – **Billy Birmingham**, *creator of the popular* Twelfth Man *recordings*

BANGLADESH

"English bookmakers had rated Pakistan 33 to 1 on, and there were no reports of unusual betting, but inevitably there were rumours about the subcontinent's illegal bookmakers" – **Wisden** *on Bangladesh's shock victory over Pakistan at the 1999 World Cup. Pakistan conceded 40 in extras and suffered three run-outs*

"A particular standard should be maintained, otherwise spectators and television will lose interest. Who will want to watch an ATP [tennis] tournament final between a player ranked 495 against one ranked 520?" – *South Africa batsman* **Barry Richards** *expresses concern about the prospect of games such as Bangladesh v Zimbabwe diluting the international calendar*

"We are not habituated to playing so long and this was the main problem" – *Bangladesh captain* **Naimur Rahman** *explains why his side collapsed to 91 all out in the second innings of their inaugural Test, against India in 2000-01, having reached 400 first time round*

"Those who learn from this match will stay and those who do not learn will not play Test cricket for long" – *Harsh warning from Bangladesh coach* **Sarwar Imran** *after India's nine-wicket win*

"His claim of being an all-rounder is clearly more a reflection of his physique than abilities" – *The* **New Age** *newspaper pulls no punches on captain Khaled Mahmud in 2003*

"One problem is television back in Bangladesh. I think players are influenced by watching India and Pakistan players like Tendulkar and Inzamam hitting the ball all over the place in matches" – *Blame TV: the Bangladesh coach* **Eddie Barlow** *clearly did*

"Everything went totally blank for me when the match was over. I can't remember what happened during those three or four minutes" – *Habibul* **Bashar** *suffers a strange blackout after Bangladesh's maiden Test win, over Zimbabwe, in January 2005*

"And to think every one of those wickets is worth the same as Bradman's in the record books" – *Alec Bedser, who dismissed the Don six times in Tests, watches with gritted teeth as England pulverise Bangladesh by an innings and 261 runs at Lord's in 2005*

"We can only beat what's put in front of us" – *England captain* **Michael Vaughan** *makes no apologies for scoring 120 in the same game*

"Like a trollop" – *England swing bowler* **Matthew Hoggard**, *asked how he bowled after taking eight wickets to defeat Bangladesh by an innings and 27 in the next game at Chester-le-Street*

"Are you Bangladesh in disguise?" – *England fans taunt Australia in 2005*

"Bangladesh call up nobodies" – *New Zealand TV is not quaking in its boots ahead of Bangladesh's visit*

ENGLAND

"Cricket is a game which the English, not being a spiritual people, have invented in order to give themselves some conception of eternity" – *Tory politician Lord Mancroft*

"There can be no summer in this land without cricket" – *Writer and critic Neville Cardus*

"Cricket is not so much a game as an extension of being English: a gallimaufry of paradoxes, contradictions, frightening logic and sheer impossibilities, of gentle courtesy and rough violence" – *Cricket writer Ryder Rowland*

"The England cricket team has always been a bit of a joke. That is its fascination" – *Journalist Matthew Engel*

"There are other things than games, and England is not ruined just because sinewy brown men from a distant colony sometimes hit a ball oftener than our men do" – *Novelist JB Priestley*

"It's typical of English cricket. A tree gets in the way for 200 years and, when it falls down, instead of cheering they plant a new one" – *Australia fast bowler turned administrator David Gilbert on the new lime tree inside the boundary at Canterbury*

"The laws of cricket tell of the English love of compromise between a particular freedom and a general orderliness, or legality" – *Neville Cardus*

"The birthright of British boys, old and young, as habeas corpus and trial by jury are of British men" – *Arthur, in Thomas Hughes's* Tom Brown's School Days

"I should challenge the Englishness of any man who could walk down a country lane, come unexpectedly on a cricket match, and not lean over the fence and watch for a while" – *Neville Cardus*

THE QUEEN (AND HER SISTER)

"G'day" – *Australia fast bowler **Dennis Lillee** meets the Queen at Lord's in 1972*

"Jeez, Henry, she hasn't got bad legs for an old Sheila, has she?" – ***Rodney Hogg** to Geoff 'Henry' Lawson as the Australians prepare to meet the Queen in 1981. Lawson claimed Hogg's compliment "could have been heard at Buckingham Palace"*

"There's a woman in the Committee Room"
"Jim, Jim, it's Saturday, it's a Lord's Test, it's the Queen"
"Nevertheless!" – *An MCC member tries to placate Jim Swanton, as recounted by **Stephen Fry** in a speech to the club*

"Nice place, Buckingham Palace. The Queen has clearly done very well for herself" – *Seamer **Matthew Hoggard** takes a look round as England celebrate their 2005 Ashes win*

"I don't care if it's the Queen of England. I'm having a night in"
"It's not the Queen of England, but it is her sister Margaret" – *Australia's matinee-idol all-rounder **Keith Miller** in conversation through his hotel door with Lord Mountbatten, the 'team liaison manager', during the 1948 Ashes tour*

"The bluest eyes I have ever seen" – ***Miller** on Princess Margaret*

"No gentleman ever discusses any relationship with a lady" – ***Miller** bats away rumours of a romance with the Princess*

"Cricket gives expression to a well-marked trait in the English character, the tendency to value 'form' and 'style' more highly than success. In the eyes of any true cricket-lover it is possible for an innings of 10 runs to be better (i.e., more elegant) than an innings of 100 runs" – *George Orwell*

"Pray God no professional will ever captain England" – *Lord Hawke keeps his fingers crossed that the amateur cricketer will always be at hand*

"How are you then?"
"It's hard work"
"Aye, and what's more you're not getting paid, are you?" – *Conversation between* **Len Hutton**, *England's first professional captain, and his batting partner* **Colin Cowdrey**, *an amateur*

"I felt rather like a head boy called to a meeting of housemaster" – *Hutton describes his impotence during a selection meeting*

"Here, everyone loves a loser" – *England captain* **Nasser Hussain** *on the essential problem with English cricket*

"It is only the players and the cricket that keeps me going. I am going to have to throw myself into cricket. If I have to think about the authorities, I will go round in circles" – *Hussain on his disillusionment with the Zimbabwe situation at the 2003 World Cup*

"If something happens, Michael, and you lead a side out there and someone gets killed, it will tarnish English cricket and your name for a long while" – *Hussain to his successor, Michael Vaughan, on the perils of leading England to Zimbabwe in 2004*

"I had more sleepless nights than when I first learnt I had cancer" – **Michael Soper**, *during his time as deputy chairman of the ECB, on the Zimbabwe fiasco*

"You might remember me. I was captain of England when they were crap" – *Hussain receives an award at the Asian Sports Personality of the Year Awards*

"Before I joined Channel 4 I played for a team that won f*** all for 15 years" – **Mike Atherton**, *who won 13 and lost 21 of his 54 Tests as captain, accepts an award on behalf of the Channel 4/Sunset+Vine cricket team in 2006*

"We're a soft touch in this country" – *Seven-times England captain and professional Yorkshireman* **Brian Close**

"There is no limit to what England cricketers can achieve, as long as you keep them off a cricket pitch" – *Giles Smith in* The Times

"Thatcher out"
"Lbw b Alderman" – *Even graffiti artists – in 1989, the year Terry Alderman kept trapping Graham Gooch plumb in front – get the joke*

"Like any Englishman armed with a cricket bat, he was doomed to fail" – *Guy Ladenburg makes his case for the prosecution after Paul Kelleher tried to decapitate a statue of Margaret Thatcher at London's Guildhall with a cricket bat in 2002*

"There is still a 'we rule the world' mentality in sections of [English] cricket. Consequently there's never been a full-throated admission that England is playing crap" – *Ian Chappell in 1998, a year before England slipped to the bottom of the* Wisden *world rankings*

"England's ability to over-theorise and complicate the game of cricket is legendary" – *Chappell again*

"I love coming to dinners like this because I always know that, however old I am, I will always be just about the youngest person in the room" – *Stephen Fry addresses the MCC in 2007*

"On the last day of this tour I'm going to get one of Gough's tattoos with three lions and my number underneath it. That's not a Christmas present – it's with you for the rest of your life, so no one can take it away from me and say I'm not English" – *Kevin Pietersen, speaking on tour in his native South Africa in early 2005, explains that a tattoo is for life…*

"There is a lot of mediocrity that people settle for in England in terms of county cricket and the comfort zones of international cricket. But I am not one for settling for mediocrity, that is far from my thoughts" – *Pietersen in India during his eventful 157-day stint as captain*

"I said: 'Excuse me?!' They said: 'We've accepted your resignation.' I said: 'On what basis has it been accepted?' They had no answer" – *Pietersen recounts the gist of his phone call with England managing director Hugh Morris after he told the ECB he couldn't work with the coach Peter Moores*

"I'm just hurt, disappointed and upset that a childhood dream has been taken away from me" – *Pietersen again*

"I knew a tenure could be ended by one bad report, one incident, one bit of foul language" – *Tony Greig, another South African-born England captain, with a prophetic warning many years earlier*

"That's a load of crap" – *Michael Vaughan is self-effacing about his rating as the world's No. 1 Test batsman in 2003*

"We done 'em" – *England fast bowler Simon Jones after the 2005 Ashes*

"I guess for once we've got to say to the Poms, 'Too good this time'" – *Steve Waugh, part of the Australian contingent at the 2008 Beijing Olympics, faces up to Great Britain's position ahead of Australia in the medals table*

"I am happy to finish with an Aussie in my pocket" – *Yorkshire and England seamer Darren Gough after Australia opener Justin Langer becomes his final first-class wicket*

"Now you know why the people who stump up their cash to follow England abroad every winter are known as the Barmy Army... You've got to be barmy, or at least mildly bonkers, to fly round the world watching this lot" – *Martin Johnson in the* Sunday Times *after England are dismissed for 51 in Jamaica in February 2009*

CRICKET AND FOREIGNERS

"The French cannot imitate us in such vigorous assertions of the body" – *Report in* The Times *in 1786 of a match in Paris*

"Cricket is essentially Anglo-Saxon. Foreigners have rarely, very rarely, imitated us. The English settlers and residents everywhere play at cricket; but of no single club have we ever heard [that] dieted either with frogs, sour-kraut or macaroni" – *James Pycroft in* The Cricket Field

CRICKET AND FOREIGNERS

"If the French noblesse had been capable of playing cricket with their peasants, their chateaux would never have been burnt" – *Historian GM Trevelyan*

"How can we interrupt so noble an activity as cricket?" – *Marc Joando, president of a French court, after being told that former England opener Geoff Boycott – accused of assaulting a former mistress – was absent because of commentary duties*

"*I played for England, not Europe*" – *Ian Botham takes part in an advertising campaign against replacing the pound with the Euro*

"I know what cricket is, I've seen it on TV, but I can't play" – *Maros Kolpak, the Slovakian handball player of Kolpak fame, owns up*

"How can you tell your wife you are just popping out to play a match and then not come back for five days?" – *Rafael Benítez, the Spanish manager of Liverpool FC, in 2005*

"It was a disgrace to be caught playing foreign games. We did it under assumed names and hid behind the bushes to change into our whites" – *A former Irish player tells Tony Francis about the problems of playing cricket*

"When I go past a school and see children playing I often wish I had grown up here and got the chance to learn how to play" – *German midfielder Dietmar Hamann, interviewed on* Test Match Special *in 2007*

"I only came for the cricket. I was promised net sessions, and I got net sessions and that was excellent" – *Russian chess grandmaster Peter Svidler explains why he entered a tournament in Gibraltar in 2009. He was introduced to cricket by the British chess player Nigel Short*

INDIA

"It is in the matter of patience that I think the Indian will never be equal to the Englishman" – *Lord Harris in* A Few Short Runs, *published in 1921*

"CB Fry is of the opinion that [Indians] 'have on the average a greater natural aptitude for batting than any people'" – *Pelham Warner in* The Book of Cricket, *published in 1943*

"Indians are mad about the game. Sometimes I do think they are mad. But the unbridled passion is infectious" – *Don Bradman's view, as recalled by Richard Mulvaney, the Director of the Bradman Museum*

"This makes me wonder if cricket is a religion in India? Let me rephrase it then: it's *Indian* cricket that is a religion in India" – *Batsman turned commentator Sanjay Manjrekar on the poor attendances at neutral matches in the Champions Trophy staged in India in 2006*

"Cricket in India is not a religion, as has been said, nor is one-day cricket. Only one-day cricket involving India attracts public attention" – *Wisden editor Scyld Berry plays down a myth*

"When I finish cricket in a professional capacity and get back to watching it purely for pleasure, I won't bother going to Lord's; I'll go back to India" – *John Wright, the New Zealander who coached India for five years*

"There is no more agreeable sight to me than of the whole Maidan overspread by a lot of enthusiastic Parsi and Hindu cricketers, keenly and eagerly engaged in this manly game" – *Pherozeshah Mehta, the Parsi Mayor of Bombay, in 1934*

"It will be nothing less than to mutilate the Indian spirit if cricket were to be banished from the land" – *Madras critic NS Ramaswami in 1959*

"Just because he was British in attitude did not mean he was anti-Indian. He showed the British that an Indian can beat them at their own game" – *Harshad Kumari defends her grandfather Ranjitsinhji against the charge he was an apologist for the Raj*

"We do not want to come to Lord's for ICC and just nod our heads like little schoolboys as we used to. Now we come with fully prepared plans and want to be heard as equals" – *An Indian administrator in 1996 on the changing face of cricketing Realpolitik*

"I'm very, very happy now that Asia is running the game. The English had 100 years of it and did a pretty average job" – *Australia all-rounder Greg Matthews in 2008*

"We in India make the mistake of thinking only good boys make good captains" – *Sourav Ganguly explains why he and Mahendra Singh Dhoni have been successful leaders*

"He turned up as if he was royalty. It was like having Prince Charles on your side. There were rumours he was asking people to carry his coffin for him, although he never asked me" – *Andrew Flintoff recalls Ganguly's stint at Lancashire in 2000*

"I don't know how you Indians live here" – *New Zealand's Lou Vincent*

"One of the things I love the most about India is that you walk around the back of the hotel, and there's a man who's selling peanuts on the street for one cent a month, and he holds his head so high, and is so proud, as if he was making $2 million a month" – *Australia opener Matthew Hayden does his best not to patronise the Indians on tour in late 2008*

"India is a superpower now; it is a hundred years ahead of Australia, which is no more than a village as compared to India" – *Pakistan's Wasim Akram responds to Hayden*

"I am not sure if such simulated training is going to be a help. You mean to say if we tour Australia we need to have a beer-can in our hands all the time?" – *Harbhajan Singh is amused by New Zealand's decision to train under conditions simulating the noise and din of Indian cricket grounds*

"If you get Dravid, great. If you get Sachin, brilliant. If you get Laxman, it's a miracle" – *Australia fast bowler Brett Lee repeats the words of wisdom of his former captain, Steve Waugh*

WE DON'T LIKE CRICKET

"I'm not sure how many people will play cricket once they have experienced the emotion of driving a sled down a luge track" – *Shiva Keshavan, India's only representative at the Winter Olympics in 2002 and 2006*

"Cricket is a foreign game played in white flannels ... it is not our game, wrestling is. In fact, cricket should not be played at all. What baffles me is why Indians are so bothered about watching cricket" – *Mulayam Singh Yadav, the chief minister of Uttar Pradesh*

"I believe that this game is meant for servile countries that have always been ruled by the Western world" – *Yadav again*

"I am not very popular among girls. I'm sure they run only after cricketers" – *Pankaj Advani, India's billiards world champion*

"My blood boils when everybody goes gaga over cricket" – *Indian boxer Vijender Kumar*

"I do believe that to the ordinary people of our country, games like hockey and football have [more] significance than the world of cricket" – *Prime Minister Manmohan Singh*

"Cricket has come like an atom bomb and squashed all other sports" – *Indian hockey player Leslie Claudius*

"I was pleased to see cricket victory was the third headline, when we won medal in Olympics" – *Indian Olympic Association president Suresh Kalmadi is pleased that the medal-winners from Beijing got some coverage*

"In India we get obsessed with the individuals; we love our cricketers – whether it is a Dravid, Ganguly or Kumble. And so, if anything goes wrong with them, we sometimes don't take it too well" – *Rahul Dravid on the abusive tendencies of Indian crowds*

"I am God's favourite son, he has given me all" – *Off-spinner **Harbhajan** Singh*

"Nothing bad can happen to us if we're on a plane in India with Sachin Tendulkar on it" – *South Africa batsman **Hashim Amla***

"Tendulkar is egoless, gracious God: British media" – *Headline in Indian newspaper*

"I do not think anyone can become God. I am a normal person who plays cricket" – ***Sachin Tendulkar***

"I'm learning to say hello to people" – ***Tendulkar** on the lonely life of a star, in 2004*

"I used to receive letters written in blood, but not anymore" – ***Tendulkar**, four years later*

"The archives recall not one single incriminating incident, not one drunken escapade, not one reported affair, not one spat with a team-mate or reporter. As Matthew Parris wondered of Barack Obama in these pages recently, is he human?" – ***Mike Atherton** on Tendulkar in* The Times

"After you approach him he begins to find out your financial strength. He asks you how you are going to position him and whether you can give him products that are appropriate to his standing. He is very smart. And, boy, is he connected" – *Senior Indian executive on Tendulkar's business acumen*

"Australia turn cocky Pakistan into impotent joke" – *Headline in the* Asian Age *after Pakistan lose the 1999 World Cup final*

"Three things were clear. Hypocrisy still drags the game down. The ICC remains toothless. And India, failing to learn lessons from long periods of powerlessness, are intent on throwing their newly acquired weight around at every opportunity" – *Journalist **Greg Baum** on the fractious Australia-India series of early 2008*

"Cricket has come into the category of an extraordinary game. It has begun representing the sentiments of the people. We see cricket not as just a game, but as a symbol of the nation's sentiment" – *Indian sports minister **Uma Bharti** in 2001*

"I'm finding it quite funny more than anything. Why don't they just come out and say they are scared of India and be done with it? That would shut me up. Don't give us lip-service" – *Jason Gillespie after his invitation to help coach young Australian fast bowlers is blocked by the Australian board because he has represented Ahmedabad Rockets in the rebel Indian Cricket League*

"Beijing is a lucky place for India. Now you should teach us how to play good cricket" – ***Yang Jiechi**, China's foreign minister, after the Beijing Olympics in 2008*

NEW ZEALAND

"There is no question that being a New Zealander was a bad start in a cricketing sense. We all lacked confidence at birth I guess" – *Fast bowler **Richard Hadlee** speaks for a nation*

"Season after season, cricket fans turn on their radios and television sets and settle in for another summer of humiliation" – The Dominion Post *on the masochism of New Zealand's cricket fans as they prepare to take on Australia in 2008*

"It probably dates back to the '60s and '70s when we scored about one win a decade and then spent the next decade celebrating it" – *Off-spinner turned coach **John Bracewell** on his country's lack of consistency over the years*

"If I was shipwrecked a mile from the coast of New Zealand, I'd turn round and swim past the sharks of Australia" – *West Indies fast bowler **Colin Croft** after the ill-tempered tour of New Zealand in 1979-80*

"The most disgusting incident I can recall in the history of cricket" – *Prime Minister **Robert Muldoon** following Trevor Chappell's last-ball underarm at Melbourne in 1981*

"I consider it appropriate that the Australia team were wearing yellow" – *Muldoon, still fuming*

"This has to be embarrassing for me. But there's a job to be done. I will cite the bare facts" – *Walter Hadlee after nominating his son Richard as one of Wisden's five cricketers of the 20th century…*

"Cricket to me is a job, not a sport. Enjoyment rarely comes into it" – *… and his equally single-minded son*

"I had the feeling that I could be talking to a robot. Richard seemed to be programmed from without" – *Journalist and broadcaster Tony Francis in conversation with Richard Hadlee*

"The best way to eliminate the patronising attitude the Poms have shown towards New Zealand cricket was to beat them under their own noses. The five-wicket win was like Roger Bannister breaking the four-minute mile" – *Graham Dowling, secretary of the New Zealand cricket board, celebrates after victory over England at Headingley in 1983, their first Test win on English soil*

"It didn't matter what we did, the English media couldn't see anything good in us. It was about how badly they'd played and not much else, and that ticked us off – almost to a man" – *Stephen Fleming after New Zealand had won 2-1 in England in 1999*

"We are not vigilantes, we are not holding people to ransom" – *Chris Cairns defends his side's policy of charging fans for autographs on their tour of England in 2004*

"We found Rob Nicol, the Auckland batsman, on the terraces this afternoon, luckily before he went to the bar" – *John Bracewell after New Zealand ran out of substitute fielders at Headingley in 2004*

"It's nice to play in front of a crowd who aren't suggesting you do things with sheep like they did in New Zealand" – *England off-spinner Graeme Swann returns home*

"Sometimes I wish I was Adam Gilchrist" – *Self-consciously stodgy opener* **Mark Richardson** *after a six-hour 93 at Lord's in 2004*

"I have a Test bowling average that is better than Sir Richard Hadlee's, and a 50-50 record in the end-of-series running race" – *Richardson lists his achievements after announcing his retirement a few months later*

"The South Africans really struggled to understand the principle of the whole thing. They're very competitive and they took it a bit seriously. But because I lost, it goes down in the record book as an unofficial dead heat" – **Richardson** *recalls his only defeat at the end-of-tour race against Neil McKenzie*

"He's too fat" – *Former wicket-keeper* **Adam Parore** *uses his newspaper column to criticise new kid on the block Jesse Ryder*

"I'm not fussed with what he had to say – he wasn't an angel himself, was he?" – **Ryder** *to Parore*

"Adam Parore was wrong. Jesse Ryder isn't too fat to play international cricket – he's too stupid" – *Journalist* **Steve Deane**

"The clock has been reset, he's on the road again and let's hope he and we can keep him good" – *Ryder's manager* **Aaron Klee** *promises his man will stay clear of drink*

PAKISTAN

"He looks like Groucho Mark chasing a waitress" – *Commentator* **John Arlott**'s *description of fast bowler Asif Masood*

"It's true that I have not often been out lbw in my own country. Or in England. Or West Indies. Or India. Or Australia. I play with my bat" – *Javed Miandad*

"I have never upset anyone in my life" – *Javed challenges one of cricket's most widely accepted truths*

"Thank God I shall never see the bastard again" – *Indian fan watches Javed walk off after playing his final international innings, for Pakistan v India at the 1996 World Cup*

"After Kardar's retirement, Pakistan cricket was thrown to the wolves, the cricket bureaucrats whose progeny still rule the game" – *Imran Khan on Abdul Hafeez Kardar, the father figure of Pakistani cricket*

"Some called this nepotism. I, of course, preferred to regard it as pure coincidence" – *Imran after making his first-class debut at the age of 16 for Lahore, whose chairman of selectors was his uncle, and captain his cousin*

"We were at a warm-up game in Zimbabwe once and the fast bowlers were on with the old ball. I was standing at slip with Inzi next to me. We crouched down as you do when the bowlers were coming in. Four or five balls later I noticed Inzi was still crouching and, surprised, I asked him if everything was OK. He replied, 'I'm fine, just trying to sleep. The ball is old and reversing so there's hardly a chance there will be any edges to snap up'" – *Opening batsman Aamir Sohail on fielding next to Inzamam-ul-Haq*

"They've always had a lot of talent, a lot of good players, but they're like eleven women. You know, they're all scratching each other's eyes out" – *Ian Botham on the Pakistanis*

"These Pakistanis don't know how to do anything other than argue. They never stop arguing. They are always right. And I have got to say I've almost had enough of it" – *Tony Greig watches Rana Naved-ul-Hasan and Abdul Razzaq lose it with each other in the 2008 Indian Cricket League final*

"The lack of urgency is pretty evident. Even a non-cricketing person like my wife can see that" – *Shaharyar Khan, chairman of the Pakistan Cricket Board, reacts to Pakistan's defeat to India at Multan in April 2004*

"Because they are white, I am sorry to say, and I am black, I am out of cricket and they're still playing" – *Salim Malik reckons Shane Warne and Mark Waugh got away with it as match-fixing allegations emerge at the turn of the millennium*

SHOAIB AKHTAR

"Basically, mate, my life is all about speed" – *Fast bowler Shoaib Akhtar, on himself*

"It is quite surprising that one is unfit in Pakistan and by reaching England gets fit overnight" – *Shaharyar Khan, chairman of the Pakistan Cricket Board, is piqued at Shoaib playing for Durham immediately after landing in England in 2004*

"I didn't see him in Australia because he didn't turn up for the first three days of the Test" – *England fast bowler Steve Harmison on Shoaib's laissez-faire attitude to the Super Test in 2005*

"I am the fall guy. I am always pulled up. I don't know why" – *Shoaib after being banned for abusing South Africa tail-ender Paul Adams*

"The line has to be drawn somewhere and if it is not to be drawn here, the question has to be asked: are we waiting till he commits mass murder?" – *Former Pakistan batsman Asif Iqbal after Shoaib whacked team-mate Mohammad Asif with a bat in the dressing room*

"I've realised that I'm a match-winner. But I can't do things on my own. I have to take everyone along with me" – *Shoaib and modesty*

"Shoaib Akhtar was a disaster. It was a classic case of trying to clutch something out of the burning fire. It summed the club up – a desperate measure for a desperate team" – *Former Surrey player Martin Bicknell on Shoaib's short-term signing for the club in 2008*

"He drinks alcohol, has an active sex life and he's been part of the anti-doping awareness programme" – *Former Pakistan cricketer Intikhab Alam on the crimes of Shoaib*

"Once Shoaib sees the crowds, and of course the babes around, I think he will be able to perform" – *Pakistan fast bowler Wasim Akram*

SHOAIB AKHTAR

"It looks like he's starting by the sightscreen"
"More like Astrid's front garden" – *Two locals in Balsall Common discuss Shoaib's painstaking run-up as he prepares to bowl for Birmingham League division three side Berkswell against St George's in an attempt to get fit in time for a Test match against England. He failed*

"It's evident that they have come down harshly on players from the subcontinent, while others go scot-free. Match referees do not give any favours to our teams" – *Inzamam-ul-Haq hits out at the ICC from the safety of retirement*

"My personal view is that your people are a bunch of lily-livered cowards who use one set of rules when it comes to poor Pakistan and another when it comes to India" – *A Pakistan official isn't pleased with Australia's decision to tour India in 2008, despite recent bombings, while they refused to tour Pakistan*

"Countries such as Australia and England are our allies in this war on terror, yet they are not supporting us here. Are we real allies or are we just being used?" – *Aamir Sohail*

"From economy to daily life to cricket, everything is hurt in Pakistan only because of our unnecessary involvement in war. Teams are refusing to come to Pakistan because of that war" – *Imran Khan. Pakistan did not play a Test for 14 months until Feb 2009*

"This is the end" – *Writer Kamran Abbasi after terrorists attacked the Sri Lankan cricket team en route to the Gaddafi Stadium in Lahore in March 2009*

"Thank God we decided to leave our hotel five minutes after the Sri Lankans. God forbid, had both buses been moving together it could have been catastrophic" – *Pakistan captain Younis Khan*

"Our way of life and our favourite pastime has been targeted" – *Former captain **Rameez Raja***

"Pakistan look like they will become a wandering cricket team now" – *Former coach **Geoff Lawson***

"I am extremely angry that we were promised high-level security and in our hour of need that security vanished" – *ICC match referee **Chris Broad**, whose bus also came under attack*

"The ICC must ban Broad from standing in any matches. He has intentionally tried to damage the image of Pakistan and isolate it as a cricket nation. He is twisting things. He is trying to scare away teams from playing in Pakistan" – *Pakistan's **Javed Miandad** reacts to Broad's criticism*

SOUTH AFRICA

"I must take the credit for *not* coaching Graeme – he was a freak and was best left to develop on his own" – ***Thomas Dean**, master in charge of cricket at Grey High School in Port Elizabeth, on Graeme Pollock, one of his most famous pupils*

"I swear you could have heard a pin drop" – *Opening batsman **Gary Kirsten** recalls the moment Hansie Cronje told his South African team they could make a lot of money by throwing a one-day international*

"I was arrogant enough to think I could get away with it" – *Cronje on the match-fixing scandal*

"I honestly struggled to eat and sleep … I could not find a building high enough to jump from. But I really felt bad about what I did" – *Cronje again*

"If anybody had told me in 1994 that I would play 100 Tests for my country, I would have asked them what they were smoking" – ***Gary Kirsten** announces the end of his ten-year Test career, having averaged 45 in 101 games*

"This is a guy who you know will climb Everest for South Africa" – *Former South Africa player* **Ali Bacher** *on captain Graeme Smith*

"There's nothing like putting your bare feet into fresh cow dung on a cold day. It's great" – *Fast bowler* **Makhaya Ntini** *on his early days on a cattle farm*

"If my grandfather was alive, he would have slaughtered a cow" – **Ntini** *after taking 5 for 75 at Lord's in 2003*

"I wasn't the most popular bloke in South Africa, put it that way. I did receive some nasty letters" – *Fast bowler* **Allan Donald** *after being run out with one run needed against Australia to reach the 1999 World Cup final*

"Nobody died" – **Lance Klusener**, *the batsman at the other end, in the dressing-room afterwards*

"The heart-wrenching thing was looking around the field, and seeing the Aussies' faces, and I could tell they were finished" – **Donald** *before it all went wrong*

"Shaun Pollock hadn't educated his people properly. They should have known exactly what was needed. Sri Lanka's captain Jayasuriya knew it, very well indeed" – **Frank Duckworth** *of Duckworth-Lewis fame after South Africa misread their tables at the 2003 World Cup and were knocked out by a single run – again*

"You can look at all the ifs and buts but at the end of the day it doesn't really help much" – **Pollock** *tries to be philosophical*

"I was batting in the middle. I got out, got back to the pavilion and there was a debate on. I never saw the Duckworth-Lewis paper: it was in front of the coach" – **Pollock**, *resigning the captaincy shortly after, blames the coach Eric Simons*

"The message got out on the field but it was never relayed. Nicky Boje ran out but [umpire] Bucknor chased him back. Klusener saw him but the message never got there. How we never knew we needed one more run…" – **Donald** *on the failure to alert the batsmen*

"At least I'll have two extra weeks for fishing" – *Klusener doesn't quite capture the mood … again*

"I don't think there's really time to choke, everything happens so quickly" – *Shaun Pollock looks on the bright side ahead of the World Twenty20 in 2007*

"I'd say in our environment that word is quite a laughable word, except when you are eating spare ribs or something like that" – *Graeme Smith deals with the old accusation about South Africans being chokers*

"It's amazing, there's a lady up there called Mother Cricket who doesn't sleep. It came back to haunt Michael Vaughan" – *Coach Mickey Arthur after Vaughan's appeal for a catch off Hashim Amla at Headingley was turned down. Earlier, Vaughan had been unhappy when AB de Villiers wrongly claimed a catch of his own in the slips*

"I don't think there's enough beer in all of Australia to satisfy us tonight" – *Spinner Paul Harris after beating Australia in 2008-09*

SRI LANKA

"If someone has a cute figure, they are known to have a nice Chaminda" – *Kerry O'Keeffe, Australian leg-spinner turned commentator, on Chaminda Vaas's contribution to Australian slang*

"Imagine if you got him on a triple word score in Scrabble" – *David Lloyd, Sky Sports commentator, thinks of a use for all five first names of Warnakulasuriya Patabendige Ushantha Joseph Chaminda Vaas*

"The traffic, the smog, the food – it's all very new to me. I still can't shake the feeling at dinner time, 'Is this the meal that'll do me in?'" – *Sri Lanka's Australian coach Trevor Bayliss*

"The only cricketer who's ever wound me up on the field with his antics" – *Former England captain Alec Stewart on Arjuna Ranatunga*

"Dennis Silk told me the Sri Lankan boys are playing an excellent game. They are dedicated and they mean business, while the English are like a bunch of old women" – *The president of the cricket board,* **Tyronne Fernando,** *on his conversation with the president of the MCC during England's five-wicket defeat in Colombo in 1993*

"Sri Lanka cricket at this moment of time is not going in the direction it should be going, especially with a set of muppets headed by a joker" – *Opening batsman* **Marvan Atapattu** *endears himself to his selectors as Sri Lanka struggle against Australia in Brisbane in 2007-08*

"I wasn't half the bowler he is now when I started my career" – **Muttiah Muralitharan** *on his new spinning partner Ajantha Mendis*

CRICKET AND AMERICA

"For the English, it is a point of pride that Americans cannot understand cricket. They may imbibe American movies, music, hamburgers and nuclear missiles, but their national sport remains their own" – *American cricket-lover* **Mike Marqusee**

"Cricket's cool. In five days you have time to, like, get real into it" – *Hollywood actor* **Keanu Reeves** *defends the game on* Tonight, *the American chat show hosted by Jay Leno*

"Where the English language is unspoken there can be no real cricket, which is to say that the Americans have never excelled at the game" – *Some old-fashioned snobbery from* **Neville Cardus**

"Why is that guy leaving? He can't just go – is he fed up with it?" – *Tennis champion* **Venus Williams** *watches a game in Richmond, Surrey*

"Oh, cricket? It's a fag game. What are you, nuts?" – *American comedian* **Jerry Lewis**

CRICKET AND AMERICA

"Great! Just great! ... When does it start?" – *Groucho Marx, at Lord's, asked how he's enjoying his first game of cricket*

"Are you over here on holiday, Mr Marx?"
"I was – until I saw *this* game!" – *Groucho meets the MCC secretary in the Long Room*

"In Harare a few years back, Robert Mugabe told me that he thought cricketers civilised people and he wanted Zimbabwe to be a nation of cricket-lovers. I tried explaining the game to George Bush Senior, but when I told him that it could last for five days and there might not be a positive result, I could see his eyes glaze over. I saw Bill Clinton in Moscow a few weeks ago and he asked for a copy of [my] book [on cricket]" – *Former British prime minister John Major*

"I'm a cricket match person" – *Former US president George W Bush on a trip to India*

"I was invited to Bush's ranch and when I said I had a home in Antigua, he asked me to explain cricket to him because it looks a bit like polo and baseball combined, only without the horses. We discussed it for half an hour" – *Sir Allen Stanford, in the days before he was charged with fraud*

"I am going to make a promise to the foreign minister right now and that is that I will even try to understand cricket" – *Former US secretary of state Condoleezza Rice acknowledges cricket's importance in Indo-Pakistan relations as she arrives in New Delhi*

"The President has developed his foreign policy in much the same way as a captain of a cricket team approaches an international Test match… [He] is not interested in limited overs. Instead, he has fielded a skilled and deeply experienced team that is ready for more than one-day matches" – *US ambassador to India Robert Blackwill on George W Bush's foreign policy in 2001*

CRICKET AND AMERICA

"After years of patient study (and with cricket there can be no other kind), I have decided that there is nothing wrong with the game that the introduction of golf carts wouldn't fix in a hurry" – *Author Bill Bryson*

"Sometimes, people think it's like polo, played on horseback, and I remember one guy thought it was a game involving insects" – *Clayton Lambert, West Indies opener turned coach of USA, has trouble spreading the gospel*

"Baseball has the great advantage over cricket of being sooner ended" – *George Bernard Shaw*

"Cricket is basically baseball on valium" – *Hollywood actor Robin Williams*

"Runs can be scored in several ways, like when a ball touches the ground and then leaves the playing area, or when the pair of batters (there are two on the field) run up the base line and switch places before an out can occur" – *A staff writer on Chicago's* Morton Grove Champion *paper wrestles with the nuances*

"Cricket has become something of a blood sport, performed by highly paid athletes before rambunctious crowds whose nationalist passions sometimes get the better of them" – *William E Schmidt of the* New York Times *during the bad-tempered summer of 1992, when England clashed with Pakistan*

"The captain of England's woebegone cricket team and its best bowler" – Sports Illustrated *of the USA on opening batsman Mike Atherton*

"Violence between players? Scantily clad cheerleaders? Toss in a rant by Charles Barkley and 3 minutes of commercials for every 45 seconds of actual game time and cricket may finally be ready for a mainstream American audience" – *The Los Angeles Times gets wind of events at the inaugural Indian Premier League*

WEST INDIES

"Cricket is the only unifying factor in the West Indies" – *Historian and journalist CLR James*

"He revolted against the revolting contrast between his first-class status as a cricketer and his third-class status as a man" – *CLR James on Learie Constantine*

"Who wants to make a hundred anyway? When I first went in, my immediate objective was to hit the ball to each of the four corners of the field. After that I tried not to be repetitive" – *Constantine*

"English people have a conception of themselves breathed from birth. Drake and mighty Nelson, Shakespeare, Waterloo, the few who did so much for so many, the success of parliamentary democracy, those and such as those constitute a national tradition... We of the West Indies have none at all, none that we know of. To such people the three Ws, Ram and Val wrecking English batting, help to fill a huge gap in their consciousness and their needs" – *CLR James*

"The West Indies in my view embody more sharply than anywhere Nietzsche's conflict between the ebullience of Dionysus and the discipline of Apollo" – *CLR James again*

"Burdened by those tensions which so often run like scars across the landscape of the personalities of people who come from poverty" – *Michael Manley on former prime minister of Jamaica fast bowler Roy Gilchrist*

"Any time the West Indies lose, I cry" – *Former Test-wicket-taking world-record holder Lance Gibbs*

"West Indians are not like Englishmen standing there trying to exist. They are playing shots at our best balls" – *Greg Chappell is made to think while leading Australia*

"He didn't say much so you didn't know if he hated your guts" – *Australia's Steve Waugh on fast bowler Curtly Ambrose*

"When I am at home and I see the West Indies bowling I get behind the settee to watch them" – *England and Essex batsman* **Keith Fletcher**

"You know the ring of five slips, two gullies and two leg slips or whatever is behind you in a cordon, but you never actually look at them. You just hear them" – *England opener* **Graham Gooch** *on facing West Indies' quick bowlers in their heyday*

"This is a Test match. It's not Old Reptonians versus Lymeswold, one off the mark and jolly good show" – *England captain* **David Gower** *refuses to condemn West Indies' short-pitched bowling*

"Come on, Amby, you're in the basement man, get up on the top floor" – *Australia's* **Shane Warne** *recalls how West Indies would try to get the best out of Ambrose*

"I was thankful I could walk from the crease unaided" – *England's* **John Edrich** *after some ferocious West Indies bowling at Old Trafford in 1976*

"I could have been killed. I don't think I shall ever be able to forgive [Tony] Greig for putting me in the firing line like that however much I want to play for England" – *His opening partner, the 45-year-old* **Brian Close**

"Australia were murdered, just as we were murdered, Test in, Test out, all last summer. It was like finding an old mate in the next bed in intensive care" – **Ian Wooldridge** *of the* Daily Mail *after Australia lose to West Indies by an innings at Perth in 1984*

"I bounced a cricket ball off his cheek and waited for him to fall down. He just carried on chewing gum and hit my next ball for six, 24 rows back" – *Australia fast bowler* **Rodney Hogg** *on the futility of trying to intimidate Viv Richards*

"They talk about us not having a beer with them, but it's a bit hard to come up to them afterwards and say: 'Look, well bowled. I enjoyed that one in the stomach'" – *Australia batsman* **Dean Jones** *on facing West Indies in 1988-89*

"This team cannot bat through 90 overs because they can barely sit through a feature film ... the young players probably think the Three W's was a restaurant" – *Journalist BC Pires has a dig at West Indies in 2004*

"If I had to make one comment on them, I would say that they should get rid of a little bit of bravado and concentrate on getting the cricket right. If you look bad doing it, who really gives a damn?" – *Graeme Smith, South Africa's captain, offers West Indies some advice in 2004*

"Test cricket is dead here" – *Jack Warner, the Trinidadian Fifa vice-president*

"Did I entertain you?" – *Brian Lara to the crowd at Barbados's Kensington Oval after his final international appearance*

"I'm not crazy but I talk to myself. And sometimes I answer back" – *West Indies captain Chris Gayle*

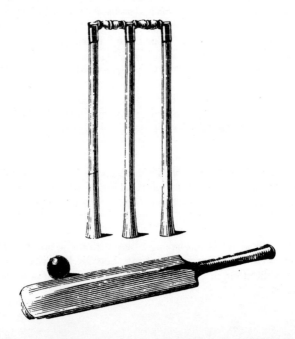

CHAPTER 4

THE PLAYERS

THE BATSMEN

"Batting is more fashionable than bowling. It has greater Fame-Value" – *Somerset seamer-turned-writer bowler RC Robertson-Glasgow*

"Not at Dorking" – *Henry Jupp, 19th-century cricketer, bowled first ball in his home town, explains why he isn't leaving the field*

"What's the good of me going in? If I miss 'em I'm out and if I hit 'em I'm out. Let's start the next innings" – *Nineteenth-century Cambridgeshire bowler (and hopeless batsman) Billy Buttress from the safety of a nearby tree*

"Get 'em swearing early and you're more than halfway to a century" – *Nottinghamshire batsman George Gunn on the pleasure he got from seeing bowlers lose their rag*

"That wasn't a bad bit of practice. I'll be able to have a go at them tomorrow" – *Don Bradman to Bill Woodfull after making 309 not out in a day against England at Headingley in 1930. He went on to make 334*

"One trembles to think what lies in store for bowlers during the next 15 or 20 years" – *England manager Pelham Warner looks on*

"I don't believe in the law of averages" – *Bradman's retort to Neville Cardus, who had the temerity to suggest he was due a failure*

"We sometimes argue about the cricketer we would choose to bat for our life. (Consensus answer: Bradman for your life, Boycott for his own)" – *Journalist Matthew Engel*

"Bradman probably sits up in the middle of the night and roars with laughter at such feeble attempts to get him out" – *Australia leg-spinner Arthur Mailey*

"One does not go seeking records. They just happen" – *Bradman*

"For God's sake, stop throwing him half-volleys – make it a bit harder for the lad!" – *Bradman, aged 73, watches an impromptu net session with the future England batsman Ed Smith, aged five*

"I think the Don was too good. I do not think we want to see another one quite like him. I do not think we ever shall" – *England batting machine Jack Hobbs on Bradman*

"He made me glad that I was not a bowler" – *Hobbs on Gloucestershire and England's hitter extraordinaire Gilbert Jessop*

"He could have made 397 [first-class hundreds] if he'd wanted but when Surrey were going well he used to throw it away, give his wicket to one of his old pals, hit up a catch and go out laughing" – *Wilfred Rhodes on Hobbs, who finished with 197 first-class hundreds*

"If you are to become a Test batsman, you must aim at solidity without fault. Absent thee from felicity awhile. Forget your dreams of brilliance and daring. Dig in, like the mole" – *RC Robertson-Glasgow*

"I don't believe in technique, I believe in performance. If you are tough, whether you have technique or not, you'll survive" – *India opening batsman Virender Sehwag*

"I've always been a slogger and my father was a slogger before me" – *England and Northamptonshire's Colin Milburn*

"Walking off after a big hundred to the applause is great, but sometimes there's a small part of me that feels a bit embarrassed" – *England and Worcestershire batsman Graeme Hick on the problem with scoring lots of runs*

"A snick by Jack Hobbs is a sort of disturbance of cosmic orderliness" – *Neville Cardus*

"When anyone asks me if I ever batted against Maurice Tate I think of the mother who asked the headmaster if her son had done trigonometry. 'Well, no madam,' replied the headmaster, gently, 'it would be an exaggeration to claim that he has done trigonometry. The most we can say is that he has been exposed to it'" – *Don Davies, briefly of Lancashire and a future football writer for the* Guardian

"Come on Richie, let's get you over with" – *England captain* **Len Hutton***'s repeated attempts to belittle the arrival into the Australian attack of leg-spinner Richie Benaud*

"Come on, let's give it some humpty" – **Ian Botham** *to England team-mate and batting dunce Graham Dilley as the pair embarked on their match-turning partnership at Headingley in 1981*

"As I was saying, I'm not a nightwatchman" – **Robin Marlar** *to Doug Insole, captain of The Rest of England, after he was stumped second ball for six at The Oval in 1955*

"I'm not sure how I'm going to cope" – **Ashley Giles** *before going out to bat against Australia at Trent Bridge in 2005. England won by three wickets*

"Get a single down the other end and watch someone else play him" – *Geoff Boycott when asked how best to tackle Australia's metronome Glenn McGrath*

"You don't need any footwork in batting – only hands and eye" – *Pakistan's* **Majid Khan**

"Staring at bowlers and mouthy fielders was one of my hobbies" – *West Indies'* **Viv Richards**

"It's a lovely day and we haven't a chance of an appeal against the light. But I can't say I feel like another over before lunch" – *Trevor Bailey to Jim Laker as England fight to save a Test against Australia. Bailey appealed anyway and the fielders trooped off*

"It shows that after 168 Tests you can still lose the plot under pressure" – *Steve Waugh* *after getting caught out on the boundary for 80 in his final Test innings, against India at Sydney in 2003-04*

"It's hard work making batting look effortless" – *David Gower*

"At one end I felt like Donald Bradman, at the other Donald Duck" – *Ray East, after making an unbeaten 48 for Essex against a Hampshire side including West Indian quick Malcolm Marshall*

"I've never batted for so long before in my life. I've got a blister on my finger. It's my first batting injury" – *South Africa fast bowler Dale Steyn after making a shock 76 in 238 minutes against Australia at Melbourne in 2008-09*

"No. 11 is probably the toughest place to bat. There are days when I'm hitting them well and the guy at the other end gets out. There must be a massive innings coming up to even everything all up" – *Glenn McGrath (career average: 6.50) ahead of his 100th Test appearance. Three games later, he made 61 against New Zealand, which remained his highest first-class score*

THE BOWLERS

"He would lumber up to the wicket and toss up the ball in a take-it-or-leave-it style, as if he cared little whether it pitched between the wickets or in the next garden" – *Sir Arthur Conan Doyle on WG Grace*

"It ain't a bit of use my bowling good'uns to him now. It's a case of I puts the ball where I please and he puts it where he pleases" – *Seamer Jemmy Shaw on the travails of bowling to WG*

"Surely you're not leaving us, Doctor? There's one stump still standing" – *Essex fast bowler Charles Kortright to WG during a match against Gloucestershire in 1898. Grace, his middle and leg stumps out of the ground, had just survived an lbw appeal and a catch for caught behind*

"This thing can be done" – *Fred 'The Demon' Spofforth as England prepare to chase 85 to win at The Oval in 1882. They were bowled out for 77 (Spofforth 7 for 44)*

"He must have been a great bowler; but his superiority over batsmen seems to have been partly the result of facial expression" – *RC Robertson-Glasgow on the bewhiskered, brooding Spofforth*

"He stood there like some fine animal baffled at the uselessness of great strength and effort in this world" – *Neville Cardus on Tom Richardson following a 42.3-over stint in vain against Australia at Old Trafford in 1896*

"There's nothing wrong with being aggressive – the bloke down the other end has a bat, some pads and a helmet" – *England fast bowler Simon Jones*

"None of us likes it, but some of us shows it more than others" – *England and Yorkshire's Maurice Leyland on facing fast bowling*

"I never let them forget the game is played with a very hard ball" – *England fast bowler John Snow*

"I treat them like faceless, meaningless thieves" – *Australia fast bowler Dennis Lillee's attitude towards batsmen*

"It doesn't worry me in the least to see the batsman hurt, rolling around screaming and blood on the pitch" – *And that of his compatriot Jeff Thomson*

"I have searched the rule books and there is not a word in any of them that says a fellow cannot bowl a fast full-toss at a batsman" – *West Indies fast bowler Roy Gilchrist on his penchant for the beamer*

"Ray Lindwall never bowled a bouncer at me. He said that if he couldn't bowl out a No. 9 then he oughtn't to be playing for Australia" – *England spinner Jim Laker*

"Sorry, Godfrey, but I have to do it – the crowd are a bit bored at the moment" – *Australia's Keith Miller apologises to England's Godfrey Evans after sending down successive bouncers*

"They said to me at The Oval, come and see our new bowling machine. Bowling machine? I said, 'I used to be the bowling machine'" – *England and Surrey seamer Alec Bedser*

"It wasn't really as difficult as I thought it would be" – *West Indies fast bowler* **Fidel Edwards**, *after taking 5 for 36 on Test debut against Sri Lanka at the age of 18*

"Only *I* polish the ball" – **Richard Hadlee** *to Mike Gatting during the MCC v Rest of the World match at Lord's in 1987*

"You can't smoke 20 a day and bowl fast" – *England's* **Phil Tufnell** *reveals why he became a spinner*

"It's a stupid rule. Everyone in county cricket thinks that it's only been brought in to protect one batsman, and that's Graeme Hick" – *Pakistan's* **Wasim Akram** *on the new one-bouncer-per-over rule, introduced in the early 1990s*

"We've got a chap called Tyson, but you won't have heard of him because he's hardly ever played" – **Len Hutton** *talks down his England team on arrival in Australia in 1954-55. Frank Tyson finishes the series with 28 wickets as England win 3-1*

"No batsman likes quick bowling, and this knowledge gives one a sense of omnipotence" – **Frank Tyson**

"It is an honest pursuit whose rewards are gained by the sweat of the brow, and not by any underhand or surreptitious methods" – **Tyson** *again*

"I can tell by the look in their eyes" – *South Africa fast bowler* **Allan Donald** *explains how he gauges whether a batsman is up for the fight*

"I go to the cricket to see a fast bowler sticking it up a batsman. Sledging has always been part of the fast bowler's repertoire" – *Australia fast bowler* **Rodney Hogg** *after an ICC plea for better player behaviour*

"You need a bit of the bully in you to dominate as a fast bowler. A touch of the Rodney Hoggs in fact" – **Allan Donald**

"Fast bowling is for nut cases" – *Pakistan's* **Aqib Javed**

"I think those speed guns are a load of crap. Somehow the white ball goes faster – I bowled 83-84mph in the Test match, and 93mph in the one-dayers. It's crazy. I hadn't bowled a ball for ten days" – *England fast bowler **Steve Harmison***

"He needed confidence. He needed to feel appreciated. I've never seen a cricketer as low as he was. He came off the field in the Test at Old Trafford and told me he was scared. It was so sad" – *England's former fast-bowling coach **Allan Donald** recalls Harmison's state of mind during a game against West Indies in 2007*

"I find it incredible that the people who are paid large sums of money to manage him don't actually manage him" – *Former player and now commentator **Bob Willis** on Steve Harmison*

"I think I must be allergic to my passport" – ***Harmison** on his homesickness*

"He had a mean bouncer, but used to apologise next ball for bowling it" – ***Jonty Rhodes** on his South African team-mate Tertius Bosch*

"I'm not going to run in 30 yards and watch a batsman shoulder arms. It's a waste of energy" – *England fast bowler **Brian Statham***

"Sorry about that, but you have a day's rest tomorrow" – ***Statham** to his feet after bowling a 30-over spell*

"I looked into his eyes and it was like there was nobody there" – ***Graham Dilley** on Bob Willis after he took 8 for 43 against Australia at Headingley in 1981*

"Whenever he hit the stumps a broad smile came across his face which he tried to conceal. It would not interest him if somebody was caught off his bowling" – ***Arthur Carr** on his Nottinghamshire team-mate Harold Larwood*

"Doing a few raids on gang houses wasn't particularly nice and mortuary stuff wasn't great. There were a few dead bodies along the line. It puts everything into perspective. If you get hit for four, you get hit for four" – *New Zealand fast bowler **Shane Bond** on his previous career as a cop*

"I really get annoyed with this reverse swing term. It's either an outswinger or an inswinger, isn't it?" – *Ian Chappell refuses to get to grips with reverse swing*

"Spin bowling is four things. One, line and length. Two, variation. Three, using the crease. Four, using fielders. That is spin bowling" – *Pakistan leg-spinner Abdul Qadir*

"If a person is bowling from dawn to dusk, when he goes back home he should still have something left in the bag. *He* is leg-spinner. If there is nothing left, he is not leg-spinner" – *Qadir again*

"Good Lord, he's bowled me a high full-toss. Where shall I smash it? Hang on, it's a low full-toss. Not to worry. Maybe it's a half-volley. Oh no, it's a length ball and I'm groping hopelessly" – *England's Vic Marks faces Qadir for the first time*

"Am I responsible for you?" – *Cricket's Livingstone and Stanley moment as Bernie Bosanquet, founder of the googly, meets Australian leg-spinner and googly bowler Clarrie Grimmett during the 1930 Ashes tour*

"I remember Tony Lock catching one at short-leg and cursing under his breath, 'Well bowled, you bastard'" – *Godfrey Evans, England wicketkeeper, on Jim Laker's Ashes 19-for at Old Trafford in 1956*

"Even when bowling out 19 Australians in a Test match … his demeanour implied that the whole thing was a fearful chore" – *Journalist Alan Ross on Laker's performance*

"My celebration dinner consisted of a bottle of beer and a sandwich in a pub near Lichfield" – *Laker*

"Never say it is turning when you have not taken any wickets" – *Len Hutton to Yorkshire off-spinner Ray Illingworth*

"I haven't got many secrets so was happy to talk to Monty – although two hours was maybe a little long" – *New Zealand captain Daniel Vettori meets fellow left-arm spinner, England's Monty Panesar*

"I can switch on and off at will, so my effectiveness as a cricketer is in no way impaired when I crack a joke between balls" – *Essex slow left-armer and habitual prankster Ray East*

"My feet feel tired when I think of him" – *England seamer Joe Hardstaff on Don Bradman*

"Well, I'll be f**ked" – *England seamer Bill Bowes's supposed response after bowling Bradman first ball at Melbourne in 1932-33*

"They said I was a killer with the ball, without taking into account that Bradman, with the bat, was the greatest killer of all" – *England's Bodyline spearhead Harold Larwood*

CRICKET AND FOOD

"I take my lunch at 1.30" – *After being told lunch has been moved to 2 o'clock, Nottinghamshire's George Gunn returns to the crease and lets the next ball hit his stumps*

"Champagne lunches are being horribly overdone. Men do not play good cricket on Perrier Jouet… No, give us some big pies, cold chickens, a fine sirloin of English beef, and a round of brawn, washed down by good ale and luscious shandygaff" – *HDG Leveson Gower in Country Life, in 1924*

"I asked Bumble to drop me off at the chippy and I said I'll eat them on the way home because the wife will have the supper on" – *Lancashire off-spinner Jack Simmons, rotund of girth*

"I don't know what I'd make of dieticians and fitness trainers" – *Simmons, who knew very well what he'd make of them*

"The blackcurrant jam tastes of fish to me" – *Derek Randall, on tour in India, samples caviar for the first time*

CRICKET AND FOOD

"Soft but not mushy" – *The ideal consistency of* **Jack Russell***'s Weetabix during Test-match lunches, according to England team-mate* **Mike Atherton**

"If my number's up I might as well go with a full stomach" – **Peter Such** *(career batting average: 8.14) orders a cheese roll and a packet of smoky bacon crisps before facing West Indies for Leicestershire*

"It couldn't have been Gatt. Anything he takes up to his room after 9 o'clock, he eats" – **Botham** *suggests* **Mike Gatting** *did not in fact take a barmaid up to his Trent Bridge hotel room to celebrate his 31st birthday. The England selectors disagreed and sacked him*

"No, he'd burst" – **Chris Cowdrey** *to* **David Gower***, who had asked him whether he wanted Gatting a foot wider*

"If it had been a cheese roll it would never have got past him" – **Graham Gooch***, the non-striker, on* **Shane Warne***'s so-called Ball of the Century to Gatting at Old Trafford in 1993*

"Shane Warne's idea of a balanced diet is a cheeseburger in each hand" – *Australia wicket-keeper* **Ian Healy**

"My diet is still pizzas, chips, toasted cheese sandwiches and milkshakes. I have the occasional six-week burst where I stick to fruit and cereal: it bloody kills me" – **Warne** *expands his repertoire*

"We never imagined this fat, podgy kid would end up as one of the world's best bowlers" – *Australia captain turned commentator* **Bill Lawry** *on Warne*

"Nothing against Indian food and all that, but I get sick over here. Hopefully, I'm better prepared this time. I've got my protein shakes, a few tins of spaghetti, a few tins of beans, I've got some cereal. Some people don't like seafood, I just don't like curries" – **Warne***, fully prepared for a tour to India in 2004*

CRICKET AND FOOD

"The entire notion of 'fusion' cooking belongs to that category of things – along with the England Test bowler Matthew Hoggard, and digital radio – that at first appear a complete waste of space, but gradually prove themselves a useful addition to human existence" – *Journalist Matthew Norman critiques a London restaurant*

"My diet was sausages then, in no particular order, sausages, chips, sausages, toast, sausages, beans, sausages, cheese, sausages, eggs, and the occasional sausage" – *Marcus Trescothick, known to his mates as 'Banger'*

"It is named after him because the seats are wider" – *Andrew Caddick on why Trescothick has a stand named after him at Taunton, Somerset's home ground*

"I'm a thick-set guy. I can't get below 16 stone without making myself ill" – *Trescothick's Somerset team-mate Ian Blackwell*

"Aye, not bad for a fat lad" – *Andrew Flintoff after winning the match award in a one-day international against Zimbabwe in 2000*

"You could put an egg on his face and it would be fried in about two minutes" – *Warne on South Africa captain Graeme Smith*

THE CAPTAINCY

"To treat a man as an automaton is the best way to make him one, and an automaton is precisely what is not required as a cricketer" – *Ranjitsinhji*

"When I win the toss on a good pitch, I bat. When I win the toss on a doubtful pitch, I think about it a bit and then I bat. When I win the toss on a very bad pitch, I think about it a bit longer, and then I bat" – *WG Grace*

"Draws? They're only for bathing in" – *Somerset captain Sammy Woods*

"The hallmark of a great captain is the ability to win the toss, at the right time" – *Richie Benaud*

"I practise a lot" – *Pakistan captain Inzamam-ul-Haq on a spell of success with the coin*

"Great toss to win, Vaughany" – *England coach Duncan Fletcher's thought process after he hears England are batting first at Edgbaston in 2005. In fact, Australia captain Ricky Ponting had decided to bowl. England made 407 in 79.2 overs*

"His captaincy was a thing of romance as well as of science. He did things as they occurred to him, by intuition or analytical observation. They might be wrong, but they were his own" – *RC Robertson-Glasgow on England captain Archie MacLaren*

"There's only one captain of the side when I'm bowling. Me" – *England's SF Barnes*

"Oh don't give it another thought. You've just cost us the Ashes, that's all" – *Gubby Allen to Walter Robins, who had just dropped Bradman in the 1936-37 Ashes. Australia went on to win the series 3-2, having trailed 2-0*

"Try to win in two days. If you can't, lose in two days so we can have a day off" – *Colin Ingleby-Mackenzie to his Hampshire team*

"Win or lose, let's entertain or perish" – *Ingleby-McKenzie again*

"One of you bugger off and the rest scatter" – *Australia all-rounder Keith Miller realises his state side has taken the field with 12 men*

"Captaincy is 10 per cent skill and 90 per cent luck, but don't try it without the 10 per cent" – *Richie Benaud*

"Go on, Rich, dive in. With your luck, you won't even get wet" – *Norm O'Neill to Benaud after Australia had somehow beaten England at Old Trafford in 1956*

"If you put your head in a bucket of slops, Benordy, you'd come up with a mouthful of diamonds" – *Derbyshire fast bowler* **Harold Rhodes** *to Benaud*

"Lately pressures and frustrations have built up so much that I'm not enjoying the game anywhere near the way I did. I'm snapping at my wife and children and I'm sleeping no more than four hours a night. This has got to stop. I now find I'm playing every ball, bowling every ball and fielding every ball. I think the captaincy has cost me over 600 runs a year" – **Mickey Stewart** *decides to quit as Surrey captain in 1971*

"At one stage Hogg suggested we survey the back of the Adelaide Oval – and I don't think he had tennis in mind" – **Graham Yallop**, *briefly captain of Australia, on his relationship with fast bowler Rodney Hogg*

"My name is now eternally entrenched in the record books as the man who led his country to that ignominious hiding against England" – **Yallop** *after his weakened side lost 5-1 at home to England in 1978-79*

"Now lads, I don't want you to think that Procter is fast… He is fast, but I don't want you to think he is" – **Brian Bolus**, *captain of Derbyshire, gives his opening batsman some advice ahead of facing Gloucestershire's Mike Procter*

"Botham's idea of team spirit and motivation was to squirt a water pistol at someone and then go and get pissed" – *Yorkshire off-spinner* **Ray Illingworth**

"I'm having a toast to the first English wicket for a day-and-a-half" – **David Gower** *sips champagne at lunch on the second day of the Trent Bridge Ashes Test in 1989 with Australia one down for 300 and plenty*

"We've won it. Now we can get on with enjoying life again" – **Stuart Law** *after his Queensland side finally won their first Sheffield Shield in 1995*

"I think of you as I do Moses, who took his languishing people on an exodus" – **Jonathan Ross** *to Nasser Hussain on BBC sports quiz* They Think It's All Over

"I would look at the pitch, call over Nasser Hussain and ask him what he would do, then do the opposite" – *Mike Atherton explains what he would do if he won the toss at Brisbane. Hussain, as England captain in 2002-03, had invited Australia to bat – and conceded 492 in a 382-run defeat*

"People have said it must be disappointing to be involved in some one-sided Test wins after the excitement of the series in England, but I'm not sure I'll ever be disappointed about not being involved in a competitive series after the Ashes experience" – *Ricky Ponting refuses to say sorry after Australia thrash West Indies at Hobart in November 2005*

"It depends on the result of the first match. If we win, people will say we were fresh, if we lose, we were rusty" – *Mahendra Singh Dhoni, captain of India, on the realities of modern-day touring*

"I'm not going to be a wimp" – *Kevin Pietersen explains how he will approach his job as England captain. His failure to wimp out cost him his job after only 157 days*

FIELDING AND KEEPING

"The gum-chewing habit is very catching; and you will sometimes see a whole fielding team resembling a herd of cows at pasture" – *RC Robertson-Glasgow, years before Australian Test captains seemed contractually obliged to chew gum*

"I see they've got you down at third man again, old son" – *Arthur Milton notices that the gravestone of his former Gloucestershire team-mate Sam Cook is in a distant corner of Tetbury parish church*

"Bowl him more often. At least that way he won't be fielding" – *Ian Chappell's advice to Graham Gooch on how to handle Phil Tufnell*

"Just practise your diving skills, fall over, lie down and watch someone else chase the ball to the boundary" – *David Boon on the pleasures of fielding at forward short leg*

"[Duncan Fletcher] knows it's something that has got under our skins and I've had enough of it, and I let him know that, and most of his players too" – *Australia captain* **Ricky Ponting** *reacts to England's policy of rotating their fielders during the 2005 Ashes*

"You can't bring it back. It's gone. I'll just spend the next 20 years worrying about it" – *England spinner* **Ashley Giles** *after dropping Ponting at a crucial stage of the Adelaide Test in 2006-07. Ponting, 35 at the time, went on to make 142 as Australia won by six wickets*

"So nicknamed because of a reputed slight hearing affliction that never seemed to impair his ability to hear the faintest snick" – **Richie Benaud** *explains why Australia's Don Tallon was known to friends as 'Deafy'*

"For all that Godfrey was a cricketing Falstaff, there was a touch of Hamlet too. He thought and fretted about life more than he let on" – *England keeper Godfrey Evans captured by his biographer,* **Christopher Sandford**

"Have you gone all religious?" – *Australia captain* **Greg Chappell** *to wicketkeeper Rod Marsh after he reprieved England's Derek Randall in the Centenary Test at Melbourne in 1977*

"We can piss this, old son" – **David Bairstow** *greets fellow Yorkshireman Graham Stevenson at the crease on a balmy night at the SCG, with England needing 35 in six overs with two wickets left to beat Australia. England won with seven balls to spare*

"Never mind about Bob Taylor. Elizabeth Taylor could have done better than that" – **Ian Gould**, *struggling behind the stumps in a game for England in Christchurch, is asked whether rival keeper Bob Taylor would have done better*

"My balcony at the Pegasus Hotel was five flights up and it would have been dead easy to slip over the side. That's how low I was. I was thinking the unthinkable" – *England's* **Jack Russell** *after missing a couple of stumpings at Georgetown in 1993-94*

"I'm such a control freak that I've already organised my own funeral" – **Russell** *again*

"I hope he doesn't go on and get a hundred" – *Durham's **Chris Scott** after dropping Warwickshire's Brian Lara on 18 at Edgbaston in 1994. Lara went on to make 501 not out*

RUNNING

"We lost innumerable singles on the off-side, and I never dared to call WG for a second run to the long-field" – ***CB Fry** reflects on batting with WG Grace on his Test debut at Trent Bridge in 1899*

"Whereas the methodical runner is like a traveller who consults weather, routes and timetables, Denis was more akin to the lover of nature who, seeing a glimpse of sunshine, snatches up his hat and sets out just for the joy of life" – *Journalist **Ian Peebles** on Denis Compton's approach to the quick single*

"Say something, even if it's only goodbye" – ***Roly Jenkins** to his England captain Bob Wyatt, not renowned for his calling*

"I'll see you at lunch, Jenkins" – ***Wyatt's** po-faced reply*

"Heads" – *Gloucestershire's **Bomber Wells**, forever running colleagues out, responds to a plea to call*

"I once got run out by deep mid-on, who overtook me as I unwisely strolled to the other end" – *Somerset seamer **Bryan Lobb**, a past-master at ambling between the wickets*

EXCUSES, EXCUSES

"Sorry, Doctor, she slipped" – *Australia fast bowler **Ernie Jones** apologises to WG Grace after sending the first ball of the 1896 Lord's Ashes Test through his beard*

"If a batsman makes, for instance, three noughts in a row, he will be able to prove that it is not the batsman's fault but the result of his great-grandfather having been an unsuccessful pawnbroker" – *RC Robertson-Glasgow*

CRICKET AND LITERATURE

"Not subversive" – *The assessment of a Japanese censor on the 1939 Wisden kept by Jim Swanton during his three-year spell as a POW in the Far East*

"It is wise not to be too rude about autobiographies; you never know who has written them" – *Neville Cardus*

"No cricketer I have known has ever been able to write well" – *Former cricket correspondent of the* Daily Mail, *Alex Bannister*

"It's the most dangerous book I'll ever write" – *Sir Bernard Ingham, former press secretary to Margaret Thatcher, after his book on the 50 greatest Yorkshiremen included Len Hutton and Fred Trueman but not Geoff Boycott*

"Every time there's been a script written, I've just about done it. I suppose I'm allowed one that I don't get every now and then" – *Shane Warne misses out on the Test wicket-taking record against Sri Lanka at Cairns in 2004*

"I'll probably still be reading it on the Ashes tour next year. I'm not a fast reader" – *Speaking at a book signing for his autobiography, Andrew Flintoff reflects on the problems of being a published author*

"Apparently a recent survey found that you are never more than ten feet from someone writing a 'Freddie' biography" – *Warwickshire all-rounder Paul Smith*

"I've not read the book" – *Steve Harmison on his own autobiography*

"It must be some measure of the catastrophic decline in Australian cricket that there are blokes in the squad these days who have not even published an autobiography, let alone a barbecue cookbook" – *Australian journalist John Huxley*

"Anyone can write a book on anyone. I don't like that law" – *Shane Warne*

"No cricketer so conveys to the spectators the perplexities and frustration of man at the mercy of malignant fate. He has much in common with that golfer who missed short putts because of the uproar of the butterflies in the adjoining meadows" – *Robertson-Glasgow on Tommy Mitchell, who played five Tests for England as a leg-spinner*

"Bloody twelfth man. Only brought out my reading glasses, didn't he!" – *Nottinghamshire's* **Eddie Hemmings** *after dropping an easy catch*

"The smell on the outfield was diabolical, and it was obviously stale wee. The main worry for the fielding side was when it came to having to shine the ball" – *Hampshire wicketkeeper* **Nic Pothas** *on the state of the Old Trafford pitch following an Arctic Monkeys concert at the ground in 2007*

"I can't guarantee you I slept particularly well – I've got a lot on my mind – but I can't even use that as a reason. I was sleeping, missed the bus and was late for work. It would be cooler if I had a better story" – *Australian leg-spinner* **Stuart MacGill** *is fined after sleeping through his alarm-call in Antigua during his final Test appearance*

"There are too many bullshitters in cricket" – *England and Somerset seamer* **Andy Caddick** *sits on the fence*

COMPETITION

"I'm trying to play like Fred, not Beefy, and Fred's doing all right at the moment" – **Andrew Flintoff** *on comparisons with Ian Botham*

"As a kid I always wanted to be the best, to win everything at school. Even now when I am driving, I don't like losing to people at the lights" – **Kevin Pietersen**

"Trevor just turned his back on me and walked away" – *Willie Watson after suggesting to Trevor Bailey at Lord's in 1953 that England might go for victory. They batted out for a draw instead*

"I was prepared to be as ruthless as it takes to stuff you" – *Australia captain* **Allan Border** *to his English counterpart David Gower after Australia won 4-0 in 1989*

"We could be playing Kick a Cockroach from Here to the Wall and we'd want to be competitive" – *Australia opener* **Matthew Hayden**

"We hate to lose, and we don't like drawing – you should see our guys play tiddlywinks" – *Zimbabwe's left-arm spinner,* **Ray Price**, *explains what gets his team-mates going*

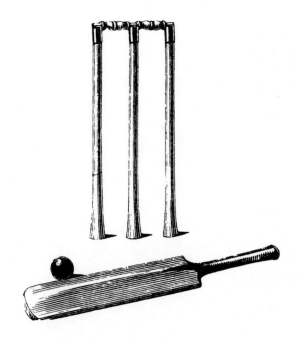

CHAPTER 5

HOME TRUTHS

BALL-TAMPERING

"You can ask any fast bowler. If he says he has never tampered with the ball, he either has just started playing, or is lying" – *West Indies fast bowler* **Michael Holding**

"Brylcreem and hair oil would also find their way on to the ball. Both were widely used as part of the fashion of the day. Of course, it was no bloody use to me. I had no hair to put it on even then" – *England fast bowler* **Frank Tyson** *on yesteryear's methods*

"Looks like Michael's trying the Aladdin's Lamp treatment" – **Tony Lewis** *on BBC TV during the Mike Atherton/dirt-in-the-pocket affair at Lord's in 1994*

"Every single bowler I know from the time I played, between 1968 and 1984, was guilty of some sort of ball-changing" – **Bob Woolmer,** *coach of Pakistan, after they were accused of tampering with the ball at The Oval in 2006*

"I personally asked every single member of the team under oath whether they had at any time scratched the ball during that innings. And to a man they said no" – **Woolmer** *again*

"They accuse us of doctoring cricket balls, with one side of the ball apparently scratched by the bowlers. Why should it be such a crime to do that?" – *Pakistan all-rounder* **Imran Khan**

"I got the 12th man to bring on a bottle top and it started to move around a lot" – **Imran** *prises open the seam – and a can of worms – during a game for Sussex against Hampshire in 1981*

"I would not have been surprised if they used knives" – *New Zealand manager Ian Taylor on Pakistan's tactics in a series in 1990-91*

"Some English bowlers who try it are usually doing it for themselves only, but Pakistan's entire match strategy is based upon getting the ball to reverse swing" – *England seamer and journalist Derek Pringle*

"Quit squealing. These two could have bowled us out with an orange" – *Geoff Boycott after England accused Wasim Akram and Waqar Younis of tampering with the ball in 1992*

"You can't accuse Pakistan of ball-tampering… The righteous indignation does make me laugh. We all know where the tampering came from, and who is best at it" – *Anonymous England player in the wake of the abandoned Oval Test of 2006*

"It took a while for word to get around the circuit but once it did the sales of sweets near the county grounds of England went through the roof" – *England batsman Marcus Trescothick on the popularity of Murray Mints as an aid to helping the ball swing*

"I think it's pretty silly of Marcus Trescothick to come out and say it, but obviously he's trying to sell some books. I think you'll find that bowlers have been doing things to the ball since cocky was an egg" – *Ian Chappell on the revelation by Trescothick that he used mint-induced saliva to retain the shine on the ball during the 2005 Ashes*

"At least now we know why England lost the Ashes: they lost their minty guy" – *Australia seamer Damien Fleming's explanation for England's Ashes defeat in 2006-07. Trescothick missed the series*

"We tried it at Lancashire. Believe me, it didn't work" – *Wasim Akram rubbishes claims that sugary saliva from Murray Mints helps the ball to swing more*

CRICKET AND INTELLECT

"Sawdust for brains" – *Pelham Warner on Albert Trott, who spent every innings at Lord's after 1899 trying to recreate the six he hit – uniquely – over the pavilion*

"If you had a head instead of a turnip, Alberto, you'd be the best bowler in the world" – *Gregor MacGregor, captain of Middlesex, to Trott*

"God had given him everything required of a bowler, except a brain-box" – *Bill O'Reilly on his Australian spin-bowling colleague Chuck Fleetwood-Smith*

"I hate speeches. As Bob Fitzsimmons once said, 'I ain't no bloomin' orator, but I'll fight any man in this blinkin' country'" – *Johnny Douglas, former Olympic boxer and captain of England, responds to the address of welcome at Melbourne Town Hall at the start of the 1911-12 Ashes. England won 4-1*

"Dam" – *Sammy Woods, captain of Somerset, writes a one-word answer in his Cambridge University finals paper. The misspelling allegedly cost him his degree*

"No good hitting me there, mate. Nothing to damage" – *Derek Randall tells Dennis Lillee why there was no point in bouncing him*

"Nowhere is it easier to pass muster as an intellectual than on the professional cricket circuit" – *Author Frances Edmonds*

"Mike said that he'd read Wilbur Smith when he was eight. That's why he went to Cambridge and I didn't" – *Graeme Hick compares his reading habits to Mike Atherton's*

"The double-first does nothing for me when I'm at the crease, I'm afraid" – *Ed Smith on the waste of a good Cambridge degree*

"The only bloke that goes well through a crisis is Warney, because I think he's as thick as a brick" – *Jeff Thomson*

CHUCKING

"In the cold light of everything, when it is looked at realistically, I must now concede that I was a chucker" – *Australia seamer Ian Meckiff*

"How was I out then – run out?" – *Essex captain Doug Insole after being bowled by Surrey's Tony Lock, whose faster ball was regarded as a chuck*

"Had I known I was throwing I wouldn't have bowled that way" – *Tony Lock after watching himself on film*

"He stands on your foot and chucks it at you" – *Unnamed England batsman on the perils of facing the giant Australia fast bowler Gordon Rorke*

"Future generations will be hoodwinked into believing 'Muchichuckalot' was the best of them all. At best, his action is suspicious. At worst, it belongs in a darts tournament" – *Broadcaster and journalist Michael Parkinson on Muttiah Muralitharan's action*

"He was bowling at three-quarter rat power. Murali's not a dill. He knows he's under scrutiny. They are filming him so he is going to do his best – and even with his best he still can't get it right. That shows there is something wrong with his action" – *Ross Emerson, the Australian umpire who once called Muralitharan for chucking, gives his views on the tests on Murali's bowling action*

"Back in Australia, when he first got called, he bowled a few leggies after that. He must be able to bowl leggies as well. He's probably just chucking that one in, sorry, putting that one in as well" – *Australia captain Ricky Ponting on rumours of a new type of delivery from Muralitharan*

"I wanted it to say 'Chuck us a VB, Murali'" – *Shane Warne on his new talking doll*

"He can't keep his mouth shut because he wants to keep making these comments. He must be a miserable man in his life" – *Muralitharan after Warne suggests the ICC assess Murali's action in a Test match*

"I thought, 'That's a load of horse crap. That's rubbish'" – *Australia wicketkeeper **Adam Gilchrist**'s reaction on being told that bowlers would be allowed to straighten their arms by 15 degrees*

"McGrath is bowling about 13, Gillespie about 12 and Brett Lee about 14 or 15, so what about them then, the Australian players? And what about other international players?" – ***Muralitharan** defends himself against claims the 15-degree regulation was brought in specifically to protect him*

"Boy George would be considered straight at the University of Western Australia" – *Former Australia leg-spinner **Kerry O'Keeffe** has little regard for the tests carried out by Perth academics on Muralitharan's bowling action in 2004*

"I definitely chucked a few but the umpires didn't pick it up and there were no TV replays. On matting wickets, an off-spin chuck got a lot of wickets" – *Former President of the ICC **Percy Sonn***

WALKING

"They're pissed off with my sudden decision to form a closer relationship with my conscience" – ***Gilchrist** receives a frosty welcome from his Australian team-mates after walking in the World Cup semi-final against Sri Lanka in 2003*

"There used to be a bloke who gave himself out by walking when he'd hit the ball. The popularity of that within his team-mates may be shown by the fact that since his retirement, they no longer reply to any emails, phone calls or text messages" – ***Gilchrist** is still bothered by his stance years later*

"You see the way Gilly throws the ball in the air. He tends to play on his walking, his honesty, but he still tries to burgle anyone and everyone" – *New Zealand opener **Mark Richardson***

"A graphic example of why so many Australian batsmen, Bradman included, have been content to leave decisions to the umpires" – *Wisden after Gilchrist wrongly gave himself out caught at slip in a one-day international against Bangladesh after the ball had flown out of a foothole*

"When Justin Langer finds his off stump akimbo he leaves the crease only after asking the Met office whether any earthquakes have been recorded in the region. In any case, he never edges the ball. It's just that his bat handle keeps breaking" – *Peter Roebuck on the Australian attitude to walking*

"In county cricket I walk, in Test cricket I don't" – *Kent and England wicketkeeper Alan Knott*

"The difference between the theory of 'walking' and the more realistic Australian or league cricket view is largely that historically in England the amateur tradition set the gentlemen above the umpires" – *Derek Birley, writer and historian*

THE BLEEDIN' OBVIOUS

"I formed the useful guiding principle that even a Demon on an evil wicket can only bowl one ball at a time, and if you really look at the ball you have a good enough chance of playing it" – *CB Fry on how to deal with Fred 'The Demon' Spofforth*

"I cling to the outworn creed that cricketers in the prime of manhood keep fit merely by playing cricket and being in their prime" – *RC Robertson-Glasgow*

"No daunting reputation of the opposition's bowlers must be allowed to make a boy forget that batting consists of playing one ball at a time, no matter by whom it is bowled" – *The MCC* Cricket Coaching Book, *published in 1963, clearly agrees*

"A straight ball has a certain lethal quality about it. If you miss it, you've had it" – *Jim Sims, the former Middlesex and England leg-spinner, gives advice to Mike Brearley*

"If the bowler happens to bowl short and fast the batsman says it is dangerous. So it is – damnably. But whose fault is that?" – *Middlesex batsman Cyril Foley*

"If the ball is there to be hit, for Christ's sake hit it" – *Somerset's Australian Bill Alley*

"Of course I would have liked to have scored 30 Test hundreds, but I might not be the person I am if I'd done that" – *Graeme Hick, possibly the most infuriating of England's many enigmas*

"A nice genuine bloke who has the habit of attracting trouble" – *Ricky Ponting on Shane Warne*

"I recently spoke to Australian captain Ricky Ponting, who told me that I should concentrate on my batting when I am at the crease" – *Ramnaresh Sarwan of West Indies works out where it has all gone wrong*

OBSESSION

"Stripped to the truth, he was a solitary man with a solitary aim" – *RC Robertson-Glasgow on Don Bradman*

"Half-hearted cricketers are rare. This game gets a grip on people such as only religious fanatics might recognise" – *Historian and writer David Frith*

"He is a queer fellow. When he sees a cricket ground with an Australian on it, he goes mad" – *Pelham Warner on Douglas Jardine, captain of England's Bodyline marauders*

"We don't play this game for fun" – *Wilfred Rhodes, archetypal Yorkshire professional and professional Yorkshire archetype*

"I didn't come out here to enjoy myself. I came out to play cricket" – *Geoff Boycott, asked by Harold Larwood whether he was enjoying an Ashes tour*

OBSESSION

"I remember going for a drink with a friend once and being asked to talk about anything other than cricket for five minutes. We stayed silent until five minutes had passed, and then got back to cricket" – *Former England batsman* **Chris Tavaré**

"When will something happen (the answer is, when you are not looking), when will it end (the day after you're gone), what is the point of it (and of life, you may well ask)?" – *Writer and journalist Alan Ross*

"He was never bored by any cricket in any circumstances; he was fond of saying that no one of any vitality, intellectual or otherwise, should know what it was like to be bored. As for being bored by cricket, that was manifestly impossible" – *Novelist* **CP Snow** *on the mathematician GH Hardy*

"I just can't think of a life without cricket" – *Sri Lanka opener* **Sanath Jayasuriya** *doesn't want to think about retirement*

"He probably just took the whole thing too seriously. That's easily done in Test cricket" – *Australia's* **Michael Bevan** *(Test batting average: 29.07) on England's Mark Ramprakash (27.32)*

THE GOOD OLD DAYS

"The elegant and scientific game of cricket will degenerate into a mere exhibition of rough, coarse horseplay" – *Cricketer turned author* **John Nyren** *in 1827 on the increasing prevalence of round-arm bowling*

"We see in action a Bradman or a Hobbs, a Jessop or a Spooner, a Frank Woolley or a Stan McCabe, or a Leary Constantine, a Walter Hammond, a Barnes (SF) or a Bill O'Reilly. But it is wiser to tuck such sights away into the happy memory than to analyse them without the labouring pen" – *RC Robertson-Glasgow*

"I didn't even wear a helmet at the battle of Tobruk" – *Sam Loxton, one of Australia's 1948 Invincibles, on modern headgear*

"I'd have looked even faster in colour" – *England fast bowler Fred Trueman*

"When I first started playing we went to the pub to talk cricket and we used to learn that way, over three or four or five pints. Now you very rarely see that. I'm old-school, so I do miss that" – *England's Darren Gough, 35 going on 70*

"I can't think why they want to kiss and hug and behave like association footballers, but they do" – *Lieutenant-Colonel John Stephenson, secretary of the MCC, on the behaviour of modern cricketers*

"Administered these days by businessmen who have no feel for, or genuine love and understanding of the game, cricket is played purely for money, ego and power for those who control it" – *BBC cricket correspondent Jonathan Agnew*

"When I first started they put the beers on ice. Now they put the players on ice" – *Australia's Darren Lehmann, ever fond of a fag and a lager, on the game's increasing professionalism*

"These days, if you're looking for a refuge from reality, Test cricket is not for you. History has invaded the pitch, with a vengeance" – *Mike Marqusee, writing in 1994*

"These days you only get to see players. They are not cricketers. In our time only cricketers played cricket" – *England fast bowler Harold Larwood in the early 1990s*

"I think one thing that a lot of people overlook is that we are not playing cricket in the 1950s and a lot of people I think are still living in the 1950s" – *Ricky Ponting stands up for the behaviour of the modern-day Australian cricketer*

MYTH-BUSTING

"I have never believed that cricket can hold Empires together, or that cricketers chosen to represent their country in distant parts should be told, year after year, that they are ambassadors. If they are, I can think of some damned odd ones" – *RC Robertson-Glasgow*

"Under the influence of topical sensationalism the defeats of Test teams have been regarded as national disasters, to the annoyance of those disinterested observers who, reasonably, doubt the sense of values of those who think the result of a cricket match means anything at all outside its immediate circle" – *Commentator John Arlott in 1953*

"That damn pitch has been rolled with heavy and light rollers for a great many years – and it won't make any difference which one is used now" – *Harold Gimblett gives his Somerset captain Ben Brocklehurst the benefit of his wisdom on rollers*

"If you are nervous when you go in first, nothing restores your confidence so much as seeing the other man get out" – *Mathematician and cricket lover GH Hardy*

"I'll tell you what pressure is. Pressure is a Messerschmitt up your arse. Playing cricket is not" – *Australia's Keith Miller*

"Concentration is sometimes mistaken for grumpiness" – *Taciturn England captain Mike Atherton*

"[Some cricketers] are like classical pianists who spend hours every day practising, whereas I'm like a jazz saxophonist who has a pretty good technique and wants to go into orbit" – *Ian Botham*

"Cricket is no more the organic outgrowth of the ancient community of the village green than Magna Carta is the work of freedom-loving Saxons" – *Mike Marqusee*

"I feel domestic cricket is tougher than international cricket. All you need to do is spend some time in the middle and runs will automatically come" – *Pakistan's **Asim Kamal** after making 73 in his third Test in 2004. He was dropped the following year having failed to score a hundred*

"Shane Warne finished 96th out of 100 in the annual *Reader's Digest* poll to find the most trusted Australian – just ahead of a convicted terrorist and a controversial Muslim cleric" – Wisden Almanack 2008

THE CLASS SYSTEM

"Yes, I drive the dust cart there every week" – *Jonah Jones, the Australian fast bowler, after King Edward VII asked him whether he had attended St Peter's College, Adelaide*

"No, sire. I was hit in the head" – *Essex and England fast bowler **Robert James** when asked by King George VI whether injuries sustained at Normandy would affect his bowling*

"Good heavens, they've asked me to captain England" – *Hon. Lionel Tennyson in 1921*

"If you learn to use a broom properly, you'll learn to use a bat properly" – *Gaby Thomas, MCC superintendent, to Denis Compton and Bill Edrich when they joined the Lord's groundstaff in the 1930s*

"About 14 – and they were all jazz hats" – *Roly Jenkins explains how many of the 183 wickets he took in 1949 fell victim of his easy-to-spot googly*

"A few of the lads, especially those from Yorkshire, haven't heard anyone speak like that before" – *England batsman **Mark Butcher** on well-spoken new team-mate Ed Smith*

"Meantime, young Trueman had to work: as a bricklayer, until he told the foreman to 'bugger off'…" – *Wisden Almanack obituary of Fred Trueman*

SAY IT AIN'T SO…

"Not very shapely. And it's masculine" – *John Arlott on the first Lord's streaker, Michael Angelow, in 1975*

"I'd much rather be known as a great guitar player than a great batsman" – *England batsman and part-time musician Mark Butcher*

"I'd rather have been a footballer" – *Michael Vaughan, a fan of Sheffield Wednesday FC*

"[I am] not a good watcher of the game. I think cricket is a boring game to watch" – *India opener Sunil Gavaskar*

"Ehsan [Mani] is a very hands-on president. I'm a hands-off president. I like to be in control too, but I don't think, of necessity, it's a president's job to do the work. That's why you have a chief executive" – *Percy Sonn prepares for office at the ICC*

"When I was batting I saw on the scoreboard South Africa had won and it made me chuckle a little bit" – *Kevin Pietersen after his native country chases over 400 to beat Australia at Perth in December 2008*

"When you've been abused as many times as I have, mate, you are bound to understand some Hindi and Urdu" – *Greg Chappell, the Australian who went on to coach India, on his linguistic skills*

"I had always laughed when playing cricket, except when the slip fielders showed signs of lumbago, and I saw no reason to stop laughing when I wrote about it" – *Robertson-Glasgow*

"Why is Tufnell the most popular man in the team? Is it the Manuel factor, in which the most helpless member of the cast is the most affectionately identified with?" – *Mike Brearley*

"What do I think of your bridge? It was built in Yorkshire by a firm called Dorman Long – and it isn't paid for yet" – *Fred Trueman to a Sydneysider*

"People say you are a long time retired but I'm taking this road now because I think if you are left out rather than going on your own terms you could end up bitter and twisted" – *Nasser Hussain explains his decision to retire in 2004*

"I don't know. You will have to ask my investor" – *Michael Vaughan, asked how many properties he owns*

"There used to be a terrible army phrase called 'man management' under which heading were set down certain elementary guidelines for handling people" – *Journalist and broadcaster EW Swanton*

"When I was young, guys like Allan Border would say stuff that made you cry but maybe cricketers these days aren't attuned to that sort of dressing-down. Nicey, nicey isn't working, so maybe it's time for something else" – *Stuart Law, who shortly afterwards was removed as captain of Lancashire*

"Cricket's the only game that has been made smaller in the past hundred years" – *South Africa's Barry Richards laments the modern tendency to bring in the ropes*

"Well played. My God, you're going to cause some problems" – *Umpire Charlie Elliott to Basil D'Oliveira after reaching 50 in the Oval Test of 1968. He went on to make 158 and earn selection for the tour to South Africa which was subsequently cancelled because of his skin colour*

"Tell him that if today's centurion is picked, the tour will be off" – *Tienie Oosthuizen, calling on behalf of the South African government, passes on a message to MCC secretary, Billy Griffith, after D'Oliveira's hundred*

"Guests who have ulterior motives usually find they are not invited" – *John Vorster, prime minister of South Africa, suggests an England team containing D'Oliveira in 1968-69 may not be welcome*

"It is not an MCC team. It is the team of the anti-apartheid movement. We are not prepared to accept a team thrust upon us. It is the team of political opponents of South Africa" – *Vorster again*

"I shed no tears when the tour was called off. I thought a dose of sporting isolation would do South Africa good" – *D'Oliveira*

"I may be black but I know who my parents are" – *Viv Richards takes on racist hecklers at Weston*

"Come on now, we're all harlots. What's your price?" – *Media tycoon Kerry Packer tries to persuade the Australian Cricket Board to part with the broadcast rights for home Tests in 1976*

"It's every man for himself and the devil takes the hindmost" – *Packer after being rebuffed by the English authorities*

"I have sacrificed cricket's most coveted job for a cause which I believe could be in the interests of cricket the world over" – *Tony Greig, then captain of England, upon joining Kerry Packer*

"Beware the small, executive subcommittee of businessmen to whom the charm of cricket is little more than a technicality" – *Journalist John Woodcock at the time of Packer*

"I have heard that the only way to get out of a contract with him is to become pregnant" – *Ray Steele, treasurer of the Australian cricket board, on Packer*

"A professional cricketer needs to make his living as much as any other professional man" – *Mr Justice Slade rules in favour of Packer at the High Court in 1977*

"We are not catering for the cricket fans. They weren't bothering to turn up to the Tests in significant numbers anyway. We are catering for the new fans, the new Australians, our audiences of tomorrow" – *Packer's PR man*

"Who made them boring?" – *Richie Benaud to the camera after Geoff Boycott, calling for four-day Tests, said five-day matches were boring*

"In real cricket, the player who has developed imagination and skill makes the game, but in the one-day match it is the other way round. The match dictates to the player" – *England captain Brian Close*

"I hate 50-over games. They're as boring as buggery" – *Fast bowler* **Jeff Thomson**

"It's so boring. You watch the start and then the overs from 20 to 40 are like pulling teeth" – *New Zealand all-rounder* **Chris Cairns** *doesn't think much of 50-over cricket either*

"I probably didn't agree with the selection" – *England seamer* **Darren Pattinson** *on his own one-off selection for the Headingley Test against South Africa in 2008*

"I think he was meant to go to Alton Towers with the kids today" – *Bemused England captain* **Michael Vaughan** *on Pattinson's selection*

"He didn't know anyone and we didn't know him, so it was very difficult" – **Vaughan**, *again, on Pattinson … again*

CRICKET AND POLITICS

"No politics ever introduced in the British Empire ever caused as much trouble as this damn Bodyline bowling" – **JH Thomas**, *cabinet secretary for the Dominions, to an audience at Claridges*

"The only group of employees more right-wing than their employers" – **Mike Edwards**, *formerly of Surrey, on the players' union in 1990*

"Scratch the surface of the average county cricketer and a nasty little racist appears" – **Frances Edmonds**

"These antis make me puke. Lefties, weirdos or odd bods – some of them may be all three" – *Glamorgan captain* **Wilf Wooller** *on supporters of a sporting ban with apartheid South Africa*

"I listen to all these republicans, and if it was down to me I'd hang 'em! I honestly would. It's a traitor's game for me" – **Ian Botham** *on the eve of becoming a knight of the realm*

CRICKET AND POLITICS

"The two things I never expected to happen in my lifetime were Sussex winning the Championship and a left-wing Labour government. As of today, a passionate Labour government is all that remains" – Playwright **David Hare** on September 19, 2003, the day his beloved Sussex finally broke their duck

"No country which has cricket as one of its national games has yet gone communist" – **Woodrow Wyatt**, former Labour MP and journalist, and cousin of the former England captain Bob Wyatt

"The cricket test – which side do you cheer for? ... Are you still looking back to where you came from or where you are?" – Tory MP **Norman Tebbit**'s notorious cricket test, laid out during an interview with the Los Angeles Times in 1990

"I'm very, very proud of my heritage – and unlike Mr Keating, I have one" – **Botham** turns on Australia's republican prime minister Paul Keating, after walking out of an evening where a drag artist took the mickey out of the Queen

"Good grief. Even the Kremlin used to get 0.1 per cent voting the other way" – **Matthew Engel** after a Daily Mirror poll reveals 100 per cent of its readers wanted Mike Atherton to resign as England captain after the dirt-in-the-pocket affair of 1994

"I fervently wished Boris would take a turn for the worse" – **Atherton** after ITN sent their news reporter to New Zealand to question his suitability for the England captaincy in 1996-97. The reporter was on stand-by to fly to Russia in case Boris Yeltsin's health worsened

"To know a no-ball from a googly and a point of order from a supplementary question is genuinely to have something in common" – Former Labour MP **John Strachey**

CRICKET AND POLITICS

"We have decided that we will each wear a black armband for the duration of the World Cup. In doing so we are mourning the death of democracy in our beloved Zimbabwe. In doing so we are making a silent plea to those responsible to stop the abuse of human rights in Zimbabwe. In doing so we pray that our small action may help to restore sanity and dignity to our nation" – *Andy Flower and Henry Olonga at the 2003 World Cup*

"We just have to be careful what we say about Mugabe. I've got no big deal about it. I'm just there to watch the cricket and I don't give a rat's arse what he does about his country" – *Dean Jones, Australia batsman turned commentator, on Zimbabwe's troubles*

"We left Downing Street and there was a lot of photographers. He said: 'What do they want?' So I looked at him and said: 'A photo, you knob'" – *England swing bowler* **Matthew Hoggard** *rubs shoulders with Tony Blair at Downing Street as part of the 2005 Ashes-winning celebrations*

"Matthew Hoggard called the Prime Minister a knob when we were celebrating winning the Ashes at a Downing Street function, and you know what? That's the first thing Hoggy's got right in a while. Blair is a knob" – *Andrew Flintoff*

"The only drinks on offer were pineapple juice and water. At the prime minister's house! Anyway, someone obviously had a quiet word and soon enough some white wine appeared. It was a bit warm, but you can't have everything I suppose" – *Matthew Hoggard*

"It's tricky to get 12 chaps on parade these days. Used to be if you scored 100, you'd get a pat on the back from the chief whip. Now your constituency chairman asks why you weren't with your constituents" – *Baron Orr-Ewing of Little Berkhamsted on the perils of arranging the Lords and Commons cricket match*

CRICKET AND POLITICS

"They have done it for cricket with the Twenty20 rules. They should now do it for Parliament" – *Tory MP Douglas Carswell wants politicians to trim down their House of Commons speeches to three minutes*

"The world must get a lesson from Obama's win, which got an African-American into the White House. That proves anything is possible and Pakistan can take inspiration from that" – *Pakistan coach Intikhab Alam looks outside the bubble*

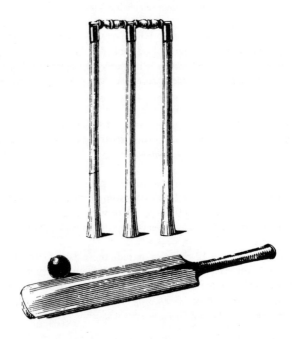

CHAPTER 6

SLEDGES

ON THE FIELD

"If I can get a batsman out by saying something that affects his game so much, then why not?" – *Shane Warne's take on sledging…*

"A totally unwelcome aberration in the game, inane, humourless and unacceptable" – *…and Mike Brearley's*

"A fine bloody way to start a series" – *England captain Walter Hammond to Don Bradman after he was given not out at Brisbane in 1946-47. Jack Ikin had claimed a catch at second slip. Bradman on 28, made 187*

"I want to hit you Bailey. I want to hit you over the heart" – *South Africa fast bowler Peter Heine to England's Trevor Bailey in 1956-57*

"Hey Randall, your mother wanted a girl and your father wanted a boy. But they had you so they were both happy" – *Australia wicketkeeper Rod Marsh to England batsman Derek Randall*

"Hospital food suit you?" – *Australia fast bowler Craig McDermott to England rabbit Phil Tufnell on a bouncy track at Perth*

"I'm going to kill you" – *Rodney Hogg to a very young Shane Warne in a club game between Waverley and St Kilda*

"Needless to say, I did not last much longer" – *Warne's reaction, metaphorically of course*

"Make sure you go this time, and don't change your mind, you South African bastard" – *Rod Marsh escorts England's Allan Lamb – born in Langebaanweg – off the field after he had failed to walk for an earlier catch*

"Does yer f**king husband play cricket as well?" – *Merv Hughes to Robin Smith, and assorted other England batsmen, during the 1989 Ashes*

"Mate, if you just turn the bat over you'll find the instructions on the back" – *Hughes to Smith*

"He offended me in a former life" – *Hughes tells umpire Dickie Bird why he is sledging Graeme Hick*

"You look like a fat bus conductor" – *Pakistan's Javed Miandad to Hughes*

"Tickets please!" – *Hughes dismisses Javed soon after*

"Didn't you go to the team meeting? They would have told you you can't bowl on middle and leg to me" – *Australia's Dean Jones to England seamer Angus Fraser after hitting him through midwicket at Trent Bridge in 1989*

"What do you think this is? A f**king tea party? No, you can't have a f**king glass of water. You can f**king wait like the rest of us" – *Australia captain Allan Border to England batsman Robin Smith at Trent Bridge in 1989*

"I've met bigger, uglier bowlers than you mate, now f**k off and bowl the next one" – *Border to Fraser*

"I was prepared to be as ruthless as it takes to stuff you" – *Border to his England counterpart and old friend David Gower once the Ashes had been won*

"A lot of people go missing in South Africa every day and one more won't be noticed" – *South Africa all-rounder Brian McMillan to Shane Warne*

"Next time you're in South Africa, I will take you fishing. And I will use you as bait for the sharks" – *McMillan to Warne, a few overs later*

"A f**king cheat, a f**king chucker" – *England captain Nasser Hussain to Sri Lanka off-spinner Muttiah Muralitharan at Kandy in 2003-04*

"It's part of the game. Normally they whinge, no?" – *Murali hits back*

"It beats Monday morning at Chelmsford, all tea and Pimm's. The amount of times Steve Waugh said to me: 'Enjoy it Nasser, this is your last Test. We will never see you again'" – *England captain Nasser Hussain reveals the secret of Australia's sledging*

"I'm not sure if he's speaking in Afrikaans or not, but I try not to listen too closely" – *England opener Andrew Strauss on South Africa fast bowler Andre Nel*

"I laughed at the opposition, with their swearing and 'traitor' remarks. Some of them can hardly speak English" – *Kevin Pietersen, born in Pietermaritzburg, South Africa, represents England against the country of his birth*

"You are not God, you are a cricketer. And I'm a better one" – *Pietersen to India's Yuvraj Singh*

"He's under pressure, he wants to go to Bangladesh"
"Actually, I'm not too keen" – *England's Graham Thorpe responds to South Africa's Herschelle Gibbs at The Oval in 2003. England's next Test was in Bangladesh*

"You're always having a go at me. You're past masters at this. Just leave me alone" – *Northamptonshire's David Capel to Warwickshire fielders*

"I can categorically state that Shane did not say anything inappropriate about my mother" – *Essex captain Ronnie Irani denies claims that Shane Warne called his mum 'a whore' during a county championship match*

"At least I have an identity. You're only Frances Edmonds's husband" – *Australia wicketkeeper Tim Zoehrer to England spinner Phil Edmonds*

"I'll get you, bloody" – *India's Eknath Solkar sledges Geoff Boycott from forward short leg*

"Daryll, I've waited so long for this moment and I'm going to send you straight back to that leather couch" – *Shane Warne to South Africa's Daryll Cullinan, who had been receiving counselling after falling to Warne several times before. This time he was out for a duck*

"Go and blow dry your hair mate" – *Shane Warne loses it with his old friend Mark Waugh during an Australian domestic match*

"We know where you live" – *Glamorgan's* **Robert Croft** *tries to unsettle Gloucestershire's Jack Russell, who was famously private about revealing his address*

"Mind the windows Tino" – **Andrew Flintoff** *to West Indian tailender Tino Best at Lord's in 2004. Moments later Best is stumped charging at Ashley Giles*

"I picked up the ball and said: 'Is this the great Graham Thorpe? Stop backing away, try and get in line mate.' He said: 'Bring it on, Besty'" – *Best, shortly before Thorpe became his first Test victim at Jamaica in 2003-04*

"I do not honestly know what he was saying, but it did not appear very friendly" – *England coach* **Duncan Fletcher** *on Ricky Ponting's asterisk-laden rant at Trent Bridge after he was run out by the substitute fielder Gary Pratt*

"We're owed one dodgy decision here, boys" – *Australia wicket-keeper* **Adam Gilchrist**, *picked up on the stump mic, has a none-too-subtle dig at the umpires at Trent Bridge in 2005*

OFF THE FIELD

"I can't think of any player who has been put off his game by verbal abuse" – *Australia captain* **Mark Taylor**

"I did not know whether I was standing on my head or heels, with the consequence that two balls later I let one go, never even attempting to play it, and it bowled me" – **Jack Hobbs**, *upset by Warwick Armstrong's Australians after being given not out at Headingley in 1909, begs to differ*

"England cheated, if by cheating you include the practice of preparing wickets to suit your own purpose" – *Australia opener* **Colin McDonald** *after England win the 1956 Ashes 2-1*

"Just remember who started this: those bastards. But we'll finish it" – *Australia fast bowler **Dennis Lillee** rages to his team-mates after being bounced out by England's Tony Greig at Brisbane in 1974-75. Lillee went on to take 25 wickets in the series as Australia won 4-1*

"People who say 'I know how you feel' are just talking bullshit" – *England seamer **Peter Lever** after hitting New Zealand tailender Ewen Chatfield on the head and almost killing him*

"Arjuna, he's probably slotting himself around at 150 kilos at the moment, is he? Swallowed a sheep or something like that" – ***Shane Warne** on Sri Lanka's amply proportioned captain Arjuna Ranatunga*

"It is better to swallow a sheep or a goat than swallow what he has been swallowing" – ***Ranatunga** hits back*

"They do nothing about blokes chucking, they do nothing about all this other stuff. They are more worried about words. That is all they are full of, words, the ICC. They always look like they are doing something but they do nothing. They are the biggest bullshitters in the world. What a waste of space" – *Australia fast bowler **Jeff Thomson***

"Malcolm has been living in Dubai for too long. As I've said before, they've got a hotel under the sea there and a ski resort in the desert. It's too far away from reality" – *Australia captain **Ian Chappell** on ICC chief executive Malcolm Speed*

"Malcolm Speed is not a man who elicits a great deal of sympathy from the cricket community. He is a cold fish, lawyerly in every respect" – ***Mike Atherton** on Speed*

"The ICC are in meltdown. This is an organisation with all the brains of a chocolate mouse" – *Geoff Boycott*

"He is talented, very talented, but he has no brains" – *Boycott on Virender Sehwag, India's aggressive opener*

"Boycott can say what he wants. He once batted the whole day and hit just one four" – *Sehwag retaliates*

"You won't get me knocking him as a cricketer, but as a man I detest him" – *Sky commentator David Lloyd on Boycott*

"He can be so rude to people that sometimes you just want to punch his lights out" – *Channel 5 front-man Mark Nicholas on Boycott*

"He has the ability to be extremely charming, and an equal ability to be a complete sod" – *David Gower on Boycott*

"He is threatening to become a bore, by reducing even the strokes he has" – *Journalist John Woodcock on Boycott's approach to batting in South Africa in 1964-65*

"His ability to be where fast bowlers aren't has long been a talking point among cricketers" – *Tony Greig on Boycott*

"The only fellow I've met who fell in love with himself at a young age and has remained faithful ever since" – *Dennis Lillee on Boycott*

"I'm completely different from Pietersen. He would turn up to the opening of an envelope" – *Andrew Flintoff on his England colleague*

"His only real weakness he has shown so far in his England career is an ability to come up with some ridiculously stupid comments, which has added great value to the dressing room" – *Andrew Strauss on Kevin Pietersen's earliest contributions to the England team*

"He's a cocky bugger and I can't stand him" – *England and Surrey seamer Alec Bedser on Pietersen*

"I found Graeme Smith's attitude pretty childish. He's a bloke who needs the game but he hasn't got many friends in it. I don't talk to Smith now. It's a waste of breath, because I don't have any respect for him" – *Pietersen on South Africa captain Graeme Smith*

"Kevin and I would get on a lot better if he kept his mouth shut" – *Smith on Pietersen…*

"I thought he was a muppet from the word go" – *… and Pietersen on Smith*

"For a few mad seconds I thought, mates or not, I'm never going to speak to that dickhead again" – *Pietersen falls out with his old mate Shane Warne on the field at Brisbane*

"He's one weird cat. He's a weirdo" – *Warne on Pietersen a couple of years later*

"When you've got a pie-chucker like Yuvraj Singh bowling at you I really don't mind. When you've got Zaheer Khan bowling from one end and you get left-arm filth like that it makes you feel really good" – *Pietersen on his rivalry with Yuvraj Singh*

"I asked a few people [what 'pie chucker' meant] and they told me it was a useless kind of a bowler. Well, a useless bowler getting him out five times, that's useless batting, I'd say" – *Yuvraj retaliates*

"I am the only guy there with some hair on my chest. Unfortunately the rest of my team are all metrosexuals" – *Australia opener Simon Katich after he and some team-mates posed for a Men of Cricket calendar*

"There are some who have changed their hairstyle more than they have scored for India" – *India veteran Sourav Ganguly on unnamed newcomers in the side*

"I can get Ponting out any time. I think I can get him even after I come post a six-month lay-off. He had a lot to say about our players and about the way we play our cricket. In fact, it is Ponting who first needs to go and learn to bat against spin bowling" – *India off-spinner Harbhajan Singh on Australia captain Ricky Ponting*

"The first time I ever met him he was the same little obnoxious weed that he is now" – *Australia opener Matthew Hayden on Harbhajan*

"I am sick of political correctness. Someone asked Hayden what he thought of Harbhajan and he gave his view. Aren't you allowed to give an opinion any more?" – *Jeff Thomson*

"Matt Hayden talks almost non-stop and he would say something across me like, 'Can't this bloke get his helmet any higher on his head?' Pretty pathetic, really, like most of their sledging"– *England and Kent batsman Robert Key*

"I have never seen an Australian team play such defensive cricket – which is a good thing for us" – *India seamer* **Zaheer Khan** *after drawing a Test at Bangalore in 2008*

"He's just happened to have a good game as well, which is pretty unusual for him" – **Ponting** *fights back*

"Aye, but he needs a haircut" – *Geoff Boycott after learning that New Zealand tailender Kyle Mills has a first-class batting average of over 40*

"He just doesn't know how to do it. He thinks he's being a hard arse but he's just not a hard arse" – *Middlesex seamer* **Dirk Nannes** *on his county colleague, the Indian left-arm spinner Murali Kartik*

"We hope you die choking on your own s*** that you speak" – *New Zealand all-rounder* **Scott Styris** *to Mark Richardson after Richardson wrote an article criticising his former team-mates*

"All those queuing up for the opening slot don't have it in them. They are all crap" – *Geoff Boycott on India's top-order dilemma in 2003*

"You say that if England give me another central contract come October that would be a waste of money. To me, you are a waste of space" – *England fast bowler* **Steve Harmison** *to Boycott*

"People who only have a passing interest in the game hear the famous Geoff Boycott Yorkshire accent and may think it gives some status to his opinions. But inside the dressing room he has no status, he is just an accent, some sort of caricature of a professional Yorkshireman" – **Harmison** *again*

"I can't let my kids watch cricket any more because of the way you behave" – *Letter writer to England wicketkeeper Matt Prior after he and colleagues were criticised for excessive sledging against India in 2007*

"I can't be blamed. After all I didn't bowl long hops and half volleys. I didn't get run out with the bat in the wrong hand" – *Andy Atkinson, Multan's English groundsman, responds to criticism from Inzamam-ul-Haq, run out for a duck, that he didn't prepare a surface to suit Pakistan's fast bowlers against India*

"I've never played a Test against Bangladesh and only one against Zimbabwe, but there are some teams out there that play them a lot. And some blokes bowl at one end all day against those sort of countries and take lots of wickets. I'm sure that whoever those people are, they might get it next year" – *Shane Warne has a none-too-subtle dig at Muttiah Muralitharan*

"They all have the wrong attitude. Look at that timid little creature Ian Bell" – *Aussie-turned-Pom Stuart Law*

"This fellow is the most overrated played I have ever seen. He looks way too heavy, and the way he's been bowling out here, he wouldn't burst a paper bag" – *Harold Larwood on Ian Botham in 1983*

"Botham only did well because all the best players had joined Packer" – *Denis Compton*

"He'd say one thing one day and then suddenly he'd be saying that the same bloke he had been pushing for a year was now complete rubbish" – *Nasser Hussain recalls Botham's contributions to England's team selection meetings*

"He was all bristle and bullshit and I couldn't make out what he was saying, except that every sledge ended with 'arsewipe'" – *Mike Atherton on Merv Hughes*

"His sledging was always more subtle and intelligent than my basic stuff. It would often take me three overs to understand what he meant" – *Hughes on Atherton*

"England deserved to win, if not from the first ball at least from the second-last over" – *Australia captain* **Lindsay Hassett** *after England regained the Ashes in 1953*

"A flat-track bully" – *New Zealand's* **John Bracewell** *on Graeme Hick*

"Someone told me the Australian bowls team has a younger average age than the cricket team" – *Zimbabwe seamer* **Heath Streak**, *speaking in 2004*

"Why our cricket board are keen on having a five-Test series when England visit India next is beyond comprehension for, without the slightest doubt, they are the most unattractive and boring side to have played cricket in India" – *Sunil Gavaskar in 2003*

"It's very sad when a good wine goes sour" – *Duncan Fletcher, England's coach, responds to Gavaskar*

"The only one who really got up my nose was Steve Waugh who spent the entire series giving out verbals. A bit of a joke really when he was the one bloke wetting himself against the quick bowlers" – *Mike Atherton remembers his Australian opposite number*

"All you Aussies are a bunch of hicks who don't know the first thing about cricket" – *Ian Botham prepares to leave Australia after being sacked by Queensland in 1988*

"A prick" – *Steve Waugh on Sourav Ganguly*

"It is disillusioning to one of my youthful loyalties to realise that the Majestic MacLaren was an extremely stupid, prejudiced and pig-headed man" – *George Lyttelton, a Cambridge University blue, on England captain Archie MacLaren*

"I can't see any reason why they should carry on like a pack of morons. Australia's been getting away with this for too long, and I admire India for the way they stood up and gave a bit back to them" – *Former Australia batsman Neil Harvey*

"Neil Harvey seems to be the hardest man in the world to please where modern cricket is concerned. And to tell the truth there is no one in our current team, and I don't think there's too many around Australia that actually sit back and listen to what Neil Harvey has got to say" – *Ricky Ponting*

"A year ago I was bowling to Adam Gilchrist and Matthew Hayden; now we're bowling to David Warner and Shaun Marsh. A big difference" – *New Zealand's Kyle Mills on the decline of Australia*

"You can abuse the Indians all day long. They just nod their heads and carry on" – *South Africa all-rounder Brian McMillan*

TEAM SPIRIT

"At least if we go down we'll take that bugger Barnes down with us" – *England captain Archie MacLaren as the Omrah steamship, en route to Australia in 1901-02, encounters difficulties in the Bay of Biscay. On board was the troublesome seam bowler Sydney Barnes*

"You know, Fender, there is no man in England whose bowling I would rather face than yours; and there is no batsman in England I would rather bowl against either" – *England captain Johnny Douglas to his all-rounder Percy Fender before the 1920-21 Ashes series. England lost 5-0*

"You couldn't captain a box of bloody lead soldiers" – *Tommy Mitchell to his England captain Bob Wyatt during the Lord's Test of 1935*

"That was the most unconscious stroke I have ever seen" – *England all-rounder Gubby Allen to Peter May after May had been dismissed in a game at Fenner's*

"Charge of unconsciousness unconditionally withdrawn" – *Telegram from Allen to May after May's century on Test debut against South Africa at Headingley in 1951*

"He had more theory than Darwin, but little practical experience to back it up" – *England fast bowler **Fred Trueman** on Ted Dexter's captaincy following the drawn Ashes series of 1962-63*

"If there is any game in the world that attracts the half-baked theorist more than cricket, I have yet to hear of it" – *Trueman again*

"Kid yourself it's a Sunday, Rev, and put your hands together" – *Trueman to the butter-fingered slip fielder David Sheppard, later Bishop of Liverpool*

"Johnny [Douglas] used to bowl them in then chuck the ball to me to chuck them out" – *England's **Cec Parkin***

"Oh, aye, I worked that out a fortnight ago. But don't tell those buggers up there" – *Geoff Boycott motions to his team-mates in the England dressing room as he tells Basil D'Oliveira he can read Australia's mystery spinner John Gleeson*

"Let's get a real Australian out here" – ***Allan Border**, a Queenslander, to Dean Jones, a Victorian, during the energy-sapping tied Test at Madras (now Chennai) in 1985-86. After making 210, Jones ended up in hospital on a saline drip*

"Jeez, Merv, that one went so far it should have qualified for frequent flyer points" – *Jones to Merv Hughes after being hit for six by Ian Botham at Brisbane*

"He's not that good. He tends to start with a four-letter word and then says a load of nonsense" – *Australia captain **Mark Taylor** on Shane Warne's sledging*

"Well, we talked about not playing rash strokes. Of course, he hears me but I'm not sure if he ever listens" – *Sachin Tendulkar talks about the advice he gave when Virender Sehwag was on 295 against Pakistan at Multan in 2004. He went on to make 309*

"When he first came into the side he fielded as though he had his hands on backwards" – ***Matthew Hoggard** on then England newcomer Alastair Cook*

"Blind cricketers are more talented than our Indian cricket squad. If our team somehow manage to become as talented as the blind cricketers, we can win not one, but as many as ten World Cups" – *India all-rounder **Kapil Dev***

"Other teams have big names, but we have only one big player in Shane Warne. The rest are average" – *Rajasthan Royals' Indian seamer* **Munaf Patel** *provides his team-mates with a confidence boost*

"Monty and I overlapped at Northants but we didn't play together much as I kept him out of the team because I could bat. He was a youngster then and while he obviously had the talent to bowl he didn't have a clue how to think about the game or about life in general. Now he can think about the game but life still remains a mystery to him" – *One England spinner,* **Graeme Swann**, *on another, Monty Panesar*

JOURNALISTS

"Bill Lawry is just a one-eyed old fart: not worth feeding or getting worked up about. Life is too short to endure Mr Greig at any hour, much less before breakfast" – *South African writer* **Telford Vice** *on the old-time commentating double act of Bill Lawry and Tony Greig*

"Without Muttiah Muralitharan, Sri Lanka's cricketers might struggle to master the owl and the pussycat if they played all week by the light of a silvery moon" – **Michael Henderson**

"The mincing run-up resembles someone in high heels and a panty girdle chasing after a bus" – **Martin Johnson** *on Merv Hughes*

"His writing was rare entertainment based on the complete reversal of the aphorism 'Comment is free, fact is sacred'" – **EW Swanton** *on Neville Cardus*

"When Ian Botham tried one at Taunton, you could unfailingly spot it from Yeovil" – **Frank Keating** *didn't think much of Botham's slower ball*

"Brearley could not bat, but how he enjoyed his walk to the wicket" – **Cardus** *on the Lancashire fast bowler Walter Brearley*

"Sometimes he seemed to treat a critical match as if it were Married vs Single at the grocers' annual picnic" – **Ray Robinson** *on Australia's left-arm wrist-spinner Chuck Fleetwood-Smith*

"Mackay is the only athlete I have ever known who, as he walked, sagged at ankles, knees and hips" – *John Arlott on dour Australian batsman Ken 'Slasher' Mackay*

"If you gave 'em the Ten Commandments, they'd cut them to four-and-a-half" – Daily Mail *cricket correspondent* **Alex Bannister** *bemoans his newspaper's sub-editors*

"Leyland's bowling is a joke, but it is an extremely practical joke" – *JM Kilburn, cricket correspondent of the* Yorkshire Post

"Players of their vintage have no aversion to biological verbs and nouns from Anglo-Saxon village vernacular long ostracised by refined society" – *Ray Robinson on the language of Ian Chappell's 1970s Australians*

"It is said he retired from cricket because TV, a new-fangled gadget in the early sixties, caught him having a quiet scratch and he decided he wanted no more of such indignities" – *Ted Corbett on Peter May*

"The idea of Larsen and Harris bowling to Goodwin and Campbell isn't calculated to cause a stampede at the turnstiles – not to get in, anyway" – *Martin Johnson watches Zimbabwe v New Zealand at the 1999 World Cup*

"The most derogatory and patronising piece I've seen written on the New Zealand cricket team" – *Gavin Larsen, the New Zealand medium-pacer, is not amused*

"Snow seems too often for comfort to agree to bowl grudgingly, as if some liberty were being taken with his contract" – *Alan Ross on England fast bowler John Snow*

"When a man who has hardly appealed for a year suddenly exercises his vocal cords every few minutes a sore throat should not be too much of a surprise" – *David Hopps with a cheeky explanation for England spinner Ashley Giles's illness in Sri Lanka in 2003-04*

"Dwayne Leverock is the physical embodiment of the World Cup's new format: vast and overblown" – *Harry Pearson on Bermuda's heavyweight left-arm spinner*

"The first time during this tour that an England fast bowler has touched 90 miles an hour" – *Unnamed journalist after Angus Fraser, then cricket correspondent of the* Independent, *is stopped for speeding by New Zealand police in 2008*

"It would not come as a shock to be told that the ECB will soon be relocating its offices from St John's Wood to a Soho pavement, and that the executive committee intends to issue its marketing executives with new uniforms. High heels, fishnet tights, long cigarette-holder and a pair of dangly earrings" – **Martin Johnson** *on the ECB's decision to get into bed with Sir Allen Stanford*

"Pietersen is the most fascinating of the present crop of batsmen, and I suspect he would say the same" – **Mike Atherton**

COMMENTATORS AND PUNDITS

"I definitely believe if any of our batsmen get out to Giles in the Tests they should go and hang themselves. But I'm confident that won't happen" – *Australia swing bowler* **Terry Alderman** *ahead of the 2005 Ashes series. Giles finished with ten wickets*

"He must enjoy playing cricket. By the end of most games he can't have any match fee left. There's aggression and aggression, but when it happens every ball it just gets boring" – **Ian Botham** *on Nel*

"He's big and rawboned and I suspect he has the IQ of an empty swimming pool" – *New Zealand wicketkeeper turned journalist* **Adam Parore** *on Nel*

"When me and Lamby were playing we weren't to be seen done up like a couple of pox-doctors' clerks prancing about. No way!" – **Botham** *is not impressed with the success of Darren Gough and Mark Ramprakash on the BBC show* Strictly Come Dancing

"Murali will complete 1,000 Test wickets, but they would count as mere run-outs in my eyes" – *India left-arm spinner* **Bishan Bedi** *casts doubt, yet again, on the legality of Sri Lanka off-spinner Muttiah Muralitharan's action*

"Great? Great who? That idiot David Lloyd? Tony Greig couldn't play either. Just because you've played Test cricket doesn't mean you were great" – *Garry Sobers on the 'greats' of cricket commentary*

"The count for the first season was 13 "sh∗ts", 14 "you b∗∗∗∗∗ds", three "f∗∗ks" and one "c∗∗t"" – *John Crilly, the director of World Series Cricket, on the oaths picked up by pitch mics during the first season of WSC*

AND A TAXI DRIVER FROM TUNBRIDGE WELLS…

"That Bob Willis, I opened the bowling at school with 'im. I was much faster than 'im an' all"

BODYLINE

"I've got it. He's yellow!" – *Douglas Jardine formulates his Bodyline theory on the notion that Don Bradman didn't like the bouncer*

"We shall win the Ashes – but we may lose a dominion" – *Jardine's former teacher at Winchester, Rockley Wilson, after Jardine was made England captain for the 1932-33 Ashes*

"We have to hate them. That's the only way we're going to beat them" – *Jardine to Gubby Allen*

"I see his Highness is a conscientious objector" – *Jardine to the Nawab of Pataudi, who refused to field in the leg-trap in the first Test at Sydney. He was dropped soon after*

"In his sheer delight at this unexpected stroke of luck he had clasped both his hands above his head and was jigging around like an Indian doing a war dance" – *Bill Bowes recalls the usually phlegmatic Jardine's response to Bowes bowling Bradman first ball at Melbourne*

BODYLINE

"There are two teams out there. One is trying to play cricket. The other is not. This game is too good to be spoiled. It is time some people got out of it. Good afternoon" – *Australia captain Bill Woodfull to England manager Pelham Warner during the fateful Adelaide Test*

"If anyone fires a pistol they'll lynch us. If one man jumps the fence the whole mob will go for us" – *England fast bowler Harold Larwood after hitting Bert Oldfield in the head at Adelaide*

"I'm getting out of here – someone will get killed" – *Maurice Tate as the crowd turns nasty*

"Larwood again the unlucky bowler" – *Newsreel footage of Larwood knocking down Woodfull and Oldfield*

"Hey, which of you b*****ds called Larwood a b*****d instead of Jardine?" – *Vic Richardson shouts his question to the Australian dressing room after Jardine demanded an apology for one of the Australians calling Harold Larwood a b*****d*

"We, Marylebone Cricket Club, deplore your cable. We deprecate your opinion that there has been unsportsmanlike play" – *Cable to the Australian Board of Control*

"It was unthinkable as it was impossible that an English team should take the field with such an accusation hanging unretracted over them" – *Jardine threatened not to lead England out for the fourth Test unless the Australian board withdrew its accusation of "unsportsmanlike" behaviour*

"Jardine is loathed … more than any German who fought in any war" – *Gubby Allen in a letter home during the Bodyline tour*

"What, give up leg-theory just because it's got 'em licked?" – *Maurice Leyland on the suggestion England should desist with their tactics*

BODYLINE

"Mummy, he doesn't look like a murderer" – *Larwood overhears a young boy talking to his mother in an Adelaide theatre*

"It is definitely dangerous, creates ill-feeling, invites reprisals and eliminates all the best strokes in batting" – **Wisden**

"I do not think there was one single batsman who played in most of those Bodyline games who ever afterwards recaptured his love for cricket" – *Australian Test batsman turned journalist* **Jack Fingleton**

"Bodyline was not an incident, it was not an accident, it was not a temporary aberration. It was the violence and ferocity of our age expressing itself in cricket – *Trinidadian historian and writer* **CLR James**

"As you all know, I am the man in Australia who has most often had the legitimacy of his birth queried…"
"Surely, sir, I still hold that honour" – *Jardine interrupts a speech by Australian Prime Minister* **Robert Menzies** *at a dinner for the Ashes tourists in 1953*

"When I bowled against Bradman, I always thought he was out to show me up as the worst fast bowler in the world. Well, I took the view that I should try and show him up as the worst batsman" – *Larwood*

CHAPTER 7

SEX, DRUGS AND ROCK 'N' ROLL

"Wally, well, yes, he liked a sh*g" – *Eddie Paynter on his England colleague Wally Hammond*

"When you're a fit young stallion on tour and a smart girl's paid to make a play for you, how can you refuse?" – *Brian Close on Ian Botham's plight at the hands of the kiss 'n' tell girls*

"It's not been a very good couple of days for me. Not only did we lose the first Test, but my girlfriend has just left me" – *Fast bowler Simon Jones after England lose to Australia at Lord's in 2005 and kiss 'n' tell revelations appeared in the News of the World*

"I've dated footballers before and I've always said I would never sell a story. But when you get offered that much money you're tempted" – *Terri Reece explains why she spilt the beans on her night with Simon Jones. (The reason? £10,000)*

"Ian Botham was my best room-mate. I never saw him" – *England batsman Allan Lamb*

"Being faithful for eight weeks isn't too much to ask, is it?" – *Simone Warne after fresh allegations about her husband Shane's behaviour during a two-month stint in England before the 2005 Ashes*

"Shane Warne is the best cricketer I ever played with, and I promise you, he doesn't abstain from sex" – *Kevin Pietersen may have the answer*

"Nobody and yes" – *Michael Vaughan reveals the answers to the two questions he says he was asked most often after the 2005 Ashes: "Who p*ssed in the Prime Minister's garden?" and "Did Kevin Pietersen sh*g Caprice?"*

"Of course it goes on, it just isn't reported" – *Vaughan on misbehaviour on tour*

"It's got nothing to do with cricket. It's all about how good you look on the beach" – *England batsman* **Mark Butcher** *on the fitness drive imposed by Vaughan when he took over as captain*

"If they had scored as many runs as they had women's phone numbers during the tour, West Indies would have won the series comfortably" – *In a leaked memo,* **Richard Nowell,** *rep for West Indies' sponsors Digicel, sums up the team's attitude on a tour of Australia*

"Realistically it's a very slim chance. It's like *Dumb and Dumber*, when the girl says, 'You've got a one in a million chance of sleeping with me,' and Jim Carrey says, 'So you're saying I've got a chance'. I live by that" – *Australia opener* **Michael Slater** *on his chances of an international recall*

"Matt is one of my closest mates and one of the reasons for my success. It's uncommon to see two men show such emotion to each other in a public arena and questions have been asked about our sexuality. I can report neither of us is homosexual!" – **Justin Langer** *on his relationship with long-time Australian opening partner Matthew Hayden*

"He looks nice actually. I quite fancy him myself to be honest" – **Nasser Hussain** *on David Beckham's braided plaits*

"No one seemed to notice much difference. They just said I was my usual self but more chirpy, and kept doing Imran Khan impressions off screen" – **Dermot Reeve** *admits he once commentated for Channel 4 after taking cocaine*

"I have no recollection of seeing the ball on Saturday and Sunday. I had to watch the match video to hear what I said" – *Reeve again*

"If I'd done a quarter of the things of which I'm accused I'd be pickled in alcohol, I'd be a registered drug addict and would have sired half the children in the world's cricket-playing countries" – **Ian Botham**

"I'm aware [Botham] smokes dope. Doesn't everybody?" – *Botham's one-time agent Tim Hudson. He was sacked for making the comment*

"Oh God. Now they're stabbing Botham in the front" – *Journalist* **Matthew Engel** *on hearing Hudson's claim*

"He's been energising the group. Everyone's asking what he's on … I probably shouldn't say that!" – **Adam Gilchrist** *on Shane Warne, who had already served his one-year ban for testing positive for an illegal diuretic*

"Jeez, that's going to be bad" – **Warne** *on the smoking ban*

"I just sat in the shower and had a coffee and a couple of cigarettes" – **Mark Butcher** *explains how he recharged his batteries during the lunch break in his 173 not out against Australia at Headingley in 2001*

"If we could stop people smoking weed we would have triple the amount of players available. If you can't give up marijuana to play for your country and reach the pinnacle of your sport then you have a serious, serious problem" – *Bermuda all-rounder* **Lionel Cann**

"Several team-mates later said that they were worried they would wake up one morning, turn on the news and find out I'd died in the night" – **Paul Smith** *of Warwickshire on his cocaine addiction*

"Brazilian footballing legend Romario said that 'between the age of 18 and 30 I don't recall sleeping'. I can identify with that" – **Paul Smith**

"When I got back to Birmingham a guy asked me if we'd won or lost. I couldn't remember" – **Smith** *again*

"Cricket's first bimbo" – **Reeve** *on Smith*

"You cannot be a great fast bowler on a bottle of ginger pop" – *Nottinghamshire captain* **Arthur Carr** *explains why Harold Larwood was often at his best after two pints at lunch*

"You boys could do with a grog" – *Australian prime minister* **Robert Menzies** *spots the hungover English tourists during the 1950-51 Ashes series and invites them up to his hotel room for some hair-of-the-dog sustenance*

"You're on tour – pour" – *Botham instructs the 20-year-old Phil DeFreitas, his nervous room-mate, on life on tour in Australia in 1986-87*

"If a guy does not drink and goes off to practise or have dinner, they think you are weird. You are not: you are different" – *Geoff Boycott*

"Better find two – one to match it now and a bloodshot one to match it in the morning" – *Northamptonshire and England batsman Colin Milburn to the nurse who was searching for a false eye after he lost his left one in a car crash*

"An ordinary bloke trying to make good without ever losing the air of a fellow with a hangover" – *Peter Roebuck on Merv Hughes*

"Seventeen-and-a-half years and if people haven't got something else to talk about then they have led a f**king boring life" – *Australia batsman David Boon to an Observer journalist who asked whether he really did drink more than 50 cans of beer on a flight to England*

"I can't see these guys would come anywhere close to drinking what my era consumed" – *Australia seamer Mike Whitney on suggestions that today's players behave worse than in previous eras*

"To be honest, Mark, I'm struggling" – *Andrew Flintoff to Mark Nicholas on the open-topped bus the morning after the Ashes celebrations the night before in 2005*

"I don't know. But I do know I've drunk them all" – *Flintoff when asked how many man of the match bottles of champagne he had won*

"Ah bloody love you, Shtubbshie. You're my bloody best mate. Ah bloody love you" – *Flintoff, a corporate guest at England v Paraguay in Frankfurt during the 2006 football World Cup, is interviewed live on the BBC by Ray "Shtubbshie" Stubbs*

"If I go out I'll do it to get hammered but I don't like alcohol" – *Kevin Pietersen*

"He said if we finished if off tonight then he'd put his Visa card behind the bar" – *Andy Caddick on Marcus Trescothick's incentive to his Somerset team-mates to complete a two-day win over Leicestershire. They failed*

"Ah, it's only Bangladesh. A little bit of fizz won't be a worry" – *Andrew Symonds justifies having a few drinks the night before a one-day international in Cardiff in 2005. His attitude almost cost him a place on the tour*

"We heard there were a few blinds rattling up there last night, but we thought it was just Andrew Symonds coming in late after another night on the town" – *Durham chief executive **David Harker** offers his thoughts on ghostly happenings at Chester-le-Street's Lumley Castle*

"We love to hate them, but he's the lump of shit, sorry, lump of cow dirt, that people are thinking of" – *An inebriated **Symonds** speaking live on Australian radio on New Zealanders in general and Brendon McCullum specifically*

"Jesse Ryder's favourite shot – tequila" – *Banner at Westpac Stadium in Wellington*

"If I have a drink in hand, I excuse myself by saying, 'I'll just get a drink' but never show up in front of that person again" – *India captain **Mahendra Singh Dhoni** on his tactics for dealing with English speakers whose accents he struggles to understand*

CRICKET AND MORTALITY

"Cricket, more than any other sport, helps a person work through the experience of loss by virtue of forcing its participants to come to terms with symbolic deaths on a daily basis" – *England captain **Mike Brearley***

"When he dies his body ought to be embalmed and permanently exhibited in the British Museum as 'the colossal cricketer of all time'" – *Australia captain **Billy Murdoch** on WG Grace*

"Bowled at last" – *Inscription on the tombstone of Richard Barlow, the great Lancashire blocker of 'O my Hornby and my Barlow long ago' fame. Barlow is said to have designed the tombstone himself*

CRICKET AND MORTALITY

"When struck, Summers reeled like a teetotum, and fell" – *Wicket-keeper William Yardley after George Summers of Nottinghamshire was hit on the head in a game at Lord's in 1870. He died four days later*

"I am off to another sphere via the small bat-drying room. Better call in a policeman to do the investigating" – *Suicide note of Aubrey Faulkner, the South African googly bowler, in 1930*

"If there is no cricket to live for, then I would rather be out of the world" – *Arthur Wills, in a letter to the coroner, after he had thrown himself under a train near Portsmouth in 1956 at the age of 35. Two years earlier, Wills – a former club cricketer in South Africa and for the Royal Navy – had been diagnosed with a brain haemorrhage*

"I love you Sachin. I was sad about reports that you would never be able to play and hence I am taking this extreme step" – *Note left by 18-year-old Deepa Vasanthalaxmi, who set fire to herself in 1999 after reading that Sachin Tendulkar might have to retire because of a back problem*

"If we don't get any response from the BCCI by November 18, we have to take the drastic step of ending our lives near Eden Gardens" – *Petition signed by the cricketers of Bihar, who threatened to set themselves on fire during the TVS Cup final between India and Australia in 2003 unless the Indian board intervened in a power struggle between Bihar's cricketing bigwigs*

"He's gone to join No. 1 now" – *The vicar at the funeral in 2006 of the Derbyshire wicket-keeper George Owen Dawkes*

"For a moment I was convinced I was dying. I knew I was in serious trouble ... I had to get help" – *England opener Marcus Trescothick faces up to his depression*

CHAPTER 8

CLICHÉ AND FAUX PAS

"We know that we worked hard and put in 100 per cent effort [at Darwin]. We will put in 150 per cent effort on Friday [at Cairns]" – *Sri Lanka's **Mahela Jayawardene** promises to give it (more than) everything in Australia in 2004*

"If I happen to play I'll put 150,000 per cent in" – *Australia's **Doug Bollinger** goes even further a few years later ahead of selection for a squad to play South Africa*

"We see that any guy that is going to try 150,000 per cent in this game is going to be someone we're going to have to respect" – *South Africa captain **Graeme Smith** is understandably wary*

"The achievement that this team has achieved is a fantastic achievement" – ***Michael Vaughan** is in little doubt after England win in Barbados in 2004*

"It's like duck off a water's back" – ***Vaughan** tries to explain how easily Kevin Pietersen will cope with being sledged in his native South Africa*

"It's a Catch-21 situation" – ***Kevin Pietersen***

"Let's get this road on the show" – *Final words of **Duncan Fletcher**'s first team-talk as England coach*

"The plan was to stick to the bowling plan" – *Fast bowler **Mitchell Johnson** blows Australia's cover*

"Our game plan is to win every game we play" – *His team-mate **Michael Clarke** commits a similar crime*

"Remember to say 'Good areas', 'Work hard', 'Keep it simple'" – *A mischievous journalist passes cliché-prone England spinner* **Monty Panesar** *a note ahead of a press conference*

"You've just got to make sure you're getting the balls … in the areas you want to get them" – **Panesar** *does his best to resist the bait*

"Areas is the way forward" – *England seamer* **Stuart Broad**

"I can understand if people feel there are negatives but we're looking at the positives. We're a positive-thinking side, we've got a positive-thinking captain and we're trying to think positively" – *England's national selector* **Geoff Miller** *takes the positives*

"It's his back. Behind his tummy" – *Australia coach* **Tim Nielsen** *reveals the exact location of Ricky Ponting's injury*

"You might not think that's cricket, and it's not. It's motor racing" – *Formula One commentator* **Murray Walker**

"Oh well, ya can't expect a leopard to change its stripes" – *Australia fast bowler* **Len Pascoe** *after watching Jeff Thomson defy team orders and bowl bouncers to Geoff Boycott*

"Yorkshire 232 all out. Len Hutton ill. No, I'm sorry: Len Hutton 111" – **Radio announcer**

"And we have just heard, although this is not the latest score from Bournemouth, that Hampshire have beaten Nottinghamshire by nine wickets" – *The BBC's* **Peter West**

"The Test match begins in 10 minutes. That's our time, of course" – **David Coleman**, *spiritual father of the commentary gaffe*

"Yorkshire gave a trial to three young players. Lowson, an opening batsman, Close, an all-rounder, and Trueman, a spin bowler" – *For once,* Wisden *gets it horribly wrong*

"The obvious successor to Brearley at the moment isn't obvious" – *Former England cricketer **Trevor Bailey***

"You run out of expletives to describe this man"
"Which particular one did you have in mind?" – ***Richie Benaud** after Chris Broad gets his vocabulary in a twist trying to shower praise on Jonty Rhodes*

"The terrorist has got another wicket" – ***Dean Jones** fails to realise the mic is on as South Africa's bearded Muslim Hashim Amla takes a catch against Sri Lanka*

"It was a silly and completely insensitive thing to say and, obviously, it was never supposed to be heard over the air" – *Jones apologises, but not before losing his job with Ten Sports*

"Fidel Castro is bowling with real aggression here" – ***Viv Richards** gets over-excited about West Indies fast bowler Fidel Edwards*

"Here's Monty Python" – ***Henry Blofeld**, commentating on* Test Match Special, *on Monty Panesar*

"Peter Moores did ring me up, but he'd got the wrong Monty. I explained I couldn't bowl left-arm spin that well but I'd very happily play" – *The Sussex opener **Richard Montgomerie** gets confused with Panesar*

"That's another appeal! No it's not, it's a replay" – ***Michael Slater** gets carried away in the commentary box at the Waca*

"If this young man does not go to the top of his calling, there will be a scandalous interference with destiny" – ***Neville Cardus** on Lancashire batsman Norman Oldfield, whose one-Test career was interfered with by Adolf Hitler*

"Tired of spam? Get advanced junk mail protection with MSN 8" – *The ringing conclusion of a piece in Sri Lankan daily* The Island *in 2003, when the subs forgot the perils of cutting and pasting articles sent by Hotmail*

"If it means cutting the finger off, if that's the worst-case scenario, if that's the last resort, I'll do that, there's no way I'm missing this" – *New Zealand's **Jacob Oram**, struggling with a finger injury, is desperate to be fit for the 2007 World Cup*

"I thought I had a smile wide enough to show that I was kidding anyway"
– *Oram after newspapers appear to take his comment seriously*

"Fine, everyone wants to play sport, but what are you really going to do?"
– *Careers master to Ian Botham*

"If Graham tried harder, he could make a successful office-boy" –
Schoolteacher to Graham Gooch

"Where exactly did it hit you?" – *Reporter to Mike Gatting, nose broken and both eyes black and blue, after being hit by Malcolm Marshall*

"What league is that in?" – *Telephonist's response after a journalist about to dictate his copy gives his name as "Basil V Easterbrook"*

"Deano!"
"He's not here, Simmo, you didn't pick him" – *Merv Hughes to Australia coach Bob Simpson at fielding practice after Simpson had shouted for Dean Jones*

"If the West Indies are on top, they're magnificent. If they are down, they grovel. And with the help of Brian Close and a few others, I intend to make them grovel" – *Tony Greig before the start of England's 3-0 defeat at home to West Indies in 1976*

"I think they really would make great cricket players. If you can turn a desert into a garden you would be an awesome cricketer because you have determination and fight" – *South African batsman Jonty Rhodes encourages Israelis to take up the game*

"Unless I'm crackers or something, I've scored a bloody sight more runs than that bearded old bugger" – *Geoff Boycott (48,426 first-class runs) on WG Grace (54,896)*

"You couldn't get a result in ten days on this pitch, let alone five" – *Ian Botham early on in the Trinidad Test of 1980-81. England soon lost by an innings and 79*

THE SELECTORS

"My God, look what they've sent me! Do they think we are playing the blind asylum?" – *England captain* **Archie MacLaren** *on seeing the names of the team given him by the selectors for the fourth Test against Australia at Old Trafford in 1902. England lost by three runs*

"Who can forget Malcolm Devon?" – *Chairman of Selectors* **Ted Dexter**, *after Devon Malcolm's Test debut at Trent Bridge in 1989*

"I am not aware of any mistakes I have made" – **Dexter**, *after picking 29 different players during England's 4-0 Ashes defeat that summer*

"I've decided to commission an immediate report into pollution levels in Indian cities" – **Dexter** *after England are hammered in Calcutta (now Kolkata) in 1992-93*

"In view of Mr Dexter's unease, I've decided to commission a report into the effect of pollution levels upon the trajectories of India's spinners" – **Kamal Nath**, *India's minister for forests and the environment*

"I think we are all slightly down in the dumps after another loss. We may be in the wrong sign. Venus may be in the wrong juxtaposition with somewhere else" – **Dexter**, *tongue placed firmly in cheek, tries another tack*

"We don't envisage chopping and changing" – **Dexter** *before the 1993 Ashes. England ended up using 24 players*

"He crossed the line between eccentricity and idiocy far too often for someone who was supposed to be running English cricket" – **Ian Botham** *on Dexter*

"It had been Dexter's singular sense of humour, expressed as light wit or sarcasm yet willfully translated as solemn statement of fact, that had brought him into terminal conflict with much of the media" – *Journalist* **Alan Lee** *after Dexter steps down in 1993*

THE SELECTORS

"What did you do, chairman, when you got into a bad trot?"
"I don't know. I never had a bad run" – *Conversation between Sussex batsman and fringe England player* **Paul Parker** *and chairman of selectors* **Peter May**

"Peter had the knack of being able to ignore completely something he didn't want to bother with" – *Colin Cowdrey on May*

"One is always a little nervous watching England bat" – *A vote of confidence from* **May**

"I expect I had better whirl my arms like a windmill" – *David Gower after being told by May he should have a higher profile as England captain*

"I have thumbed through the MCC coaching manual and found that no such stroke exists" – *May on England's use of the reverse-sweep*

"May was handsome, May was dashing, May was everything a Fifties schoolboy could ever want to be [...] It was only 30 years later when he himself became the chairman of the selectors that it became obvious he was also a bit of a twit" – *Journalist* **Matthew Engel**

"We were going to sack him anyway" – *Alec Bedser after Ian Botham stepped down as England captain in 1981*

"Have you played against Australia before?"
"You're one of the selectors who picked me after I scored 75 against them for MCC at Lord's last week" – *Graham Gooch responds to* **Len Hutton**. *Gooch duly began his Test career with a pair*

"If it gets really grey, I might become chairman of the England selectors" – *Gooch on his hair*

THE SELECTORS

"They bring him out of the loft, take the dust sheet off him, give him a pink gin and sit him there. He can't go out of a 30-mile radius of London because he's normally too pissed to get back" – *Botham on the average England selector in the mid-1980s*

"The only reason I'm not selected was the fact I did *Strictly Come Dancing*" – *Darren Gough on being ignored by England*

"I didn't see him turn a single ball from leg to off. I don't believe we will have much problem with him" – *Keith Fletcher, England's coach, after his spying mission on India's Anil Kumble, who duly takes 21 wickets as England lose 3-0*

"Sir Colin Cowardly" – *A computer error intrudes on a press release for the Brian Johnston Memorial Trust in 1996*

"If a cricketer, for instance, suddenly decided to go into a school and batter a lot of people to death with a cricket bat, which he could do very easily, I mean, are you going to ban cricket bats?" – *Prince Philip in the aftermath of the Dunblane massacre in 1996*

"I think he has to accept that he will only be called upon in certain situations. If everybody is fit, he won't play. Simple as that. Unfortunately, that is the reality of Test cricket" – *Andy Caddick has a warning for his fellow England seamer Matthew Hoggard, the man he calls the 'Andrew Bicknell' of English cricket. Hoggard finishes with 248 Test wickets to Caddick's 234*

"We've been reading what Mike Atherton says in the English newspapers about how to get Strauss out" – *Shaun Pollock to Atherton during a tea-time interview in a Test at Johannesburg. Pollock's team-mate Makhaya Ntini had just removed Strauss for a duck*

"Don't tell the English public that" – *Atherton's sheepish response*

"He's a lovely guy, that Ricky Ponting. He likes the English so much he changed the series for them with the most stupid decision he'll ever make in his life" – *Geoff Boycott on Ricky Ponting's disastrous decision to bowl first at Edgbaston in 2005*

"That night I had great difficulty sleeping. The abuse I was sure to get on the field the next day chilled me to the bone" – *South Africa's **Gary Kirsten** after trying to chat up a group of women he failed to recognise as the wives and girlfriends of the Australian team*

"Morning Geraint, how are you?" – *Sky news reporter to Paul Collingwood in 2005*

"Hansie Cronje was such a hero of mine. I liked how he did, well, the positive stuff. Not all of what he did, obviously" – *Kevin Pietersen quickly remembers himself*

"Look, it's your nation, not mine" – *Slip of the tongue from **Pietersen** after telling an interviewer he gets sent pictures of naked female admirers*

"Derbyshite to stage Twenty20 double-header" – *Slip of the keyboard in a headline on the website of the **Sheffield Star** in 2009*

CRICKET AND THE MEDIA

"Cricket would be a better game if the papers didn't publish the averages" – *Jack Hobbs, who was rarely far from the top of them anyway*

"What's it got to do with you?" – *Yorkshire seamer **Alex Coxon** to any journalist who dared ring him at home to ask him how he was*

"I'm so glad I wasn't up here when I was down there" – *Australia captain **Lindsay Hassett** in the press box*

CRICKET AND THE MEDIA

"Top cricketers are mostly men of temperament. Like painters and musicians, they walk in the heaven of praise and the hell of blame" – *RC Robertson-Glasgow*

"If you were walking down the street and a fellow said that to you, if you had any go about you at all, you'd deck him" – *Australia captain* **Kim Hughes** *on media criticism*

"You've been pissing all over me for years so I thought I'd let you know how it feels" – *Former* **Northants batsman** *tells a journalist why he had just urinated over his leg in an elevator*

"My policy was never to say anything I thought to be false, and to tell as much of the truth (as I saw it) as possible" – *England captain* **Mike Brearley**

"If I had my time over again, I would never have played cricket. Why? Because of people like you. The press do nothing but criticise" – **Garry Sobers** *to a reporter*

"Sometimes you want to call up the paper or the radio and say: 'Look, I'm working my arse off here. I'm just unlucky. That's the way it goes'" – *New Zealand fast bowler* **Shane Bond** *on his long-term injury problems*

"We players shouldn't bleat when we are unfairly criticised by the media as long as it's not libellous or untrue. We're there to be shot at and we enjoy the perks when they come along" – *England captain* **Graham Gooch**

"Generally the people out on the pitch are the ones who know how to play the game, not the people who are writing about it" – *England opener* **Marcus Trescothick**

CRICKET AND THE MEDIA

"I don't listen to people, don't watch TV and don't read newspapers. It's better to use the time to work on your game" – *India opener* **Virender Sehwag**

"Anyone who tells you cricketers don't read the papers is lying" – *Anonymous former* **England international**

"You jammy bastard"
"I'll keep conning them for a while yet" – *Balcony conversation about the media between* **Mike Atherton** *and a smug* **Nasser Hussain** *after Adam Gilchrist's generous declaration allowed Hussain's England to win at Headingley in 2001*

"Much Urdu about nothing" – *Vic Marks on the press-conference musings of Pakistan captain Inzamam-ul-Haq*

"Shut up" – *Inzamam to a reporter after being asked whether a one-day international in Lahore was fixed*

"'When people ask you what aspects of your game you are working on,' Colin Cowdrey told me once, 'say, 'Oh everything, thank you'"
– *Ed Smith*

"I didn't like to be friendly with rivals. I wanted them to feel the heat. And I didn't like reporters because you people think you know everything" – *Curtly Ambrose, who let his bowling do the talking*

"I grew up reading the newspapers back to front, but now I read the front pages first, probably because what was in the back pages earlier has now moved to the front pages" – *India batsman Rahul Dravid*

"The *News of the World* saying I've just slept with Jordan" – *Asked "What headlines would you like to be reading about yourself in 12 months' time?"* **Michael Vaughan** *gives his response*

CHAPTER 9

WOE IS ME

"Nobody is so soon forgotten as a successful cricketer" – *Prince Kumar Shri Ranjitsinhji*

"If you want one for 300 when I come in I'll see you get it. It's the only way they'll remember me" – *Australia batsman Neil Hawke to Fred Trueman, a few days before Hawke became Trueman's 300th Test victim*

"Coincidence my foot. I got out on purpose. If I'd scored less, or even more, than Don Bradman, no one would have remembered my score" – *Australia batsman Sid Barnes after making 234, the same as Bradman, against England at Sydney in 1946-47*

"The uncertainty of cricket is not always glorious or exciting. It can be disillusioning and anxiety-creating" – *England captain Mike Brearley, who later became a psychoanalyst*

"Up, breakfast, stretch, practice, play, bathe, bar, steak, bed. Same company, day in, day out" – *Ian Botham tells Peter Roebuck about the joys of touring*

"Then it hit me. This bloke was a psychiatrist. And if he was a psychiatrist, what did that make me?" – *England spinner Phil Tufnell after suffering a breakdown in his hotel room in Perth in 1994-95. He escaped through a window*

"That bloke's making me look ordinary! He's ruining my career!" – *Tufnell comes over all insecure about Shane Warne*

"I ask myself: 'What am I? I don't know what to say. So I end up putting 'businessman'. Sometimes I put 'ex-sportsman'. But 'businessman' seems to fit most of the time" – *Post-retirement existential angst from Warne, not immune to worrying himself*

"One newspaper published a list entitled 'Ten things you never knew about Shane Warne' – and I swear I didn't know five of them myself" – *Warne on the perils of being public property*

"I feel I'm on *The Truman Show*" – *Warne on his dual role as famous cricketer and tabloid fodder*

"I felt spent and worthless, like an old washing machine thrown on the tip" – *Seam bowler Simon Hughes after ending his career at Middlesex following 22 years' service*

"This will take up days when I might otherwise be sitting in the park" – *England all-rounder Chris Lewis, aged 40, on why his short-term signing with Surrey in 2008 was a good idea. The following year, Lewis was sentenced to 13 years for cocaine possession*

"This is a terrible thing, this war, Neville"
"It is, indeed, when we think of all the art and culture it has left in ruins throughout Europe. The lovely old historic buildings, the…"
"Yes, yes. I know all about that. I was thinking particularly of a new ball I had discovered. I'll never have the chance now to try it out against class batsmen" – *Australia leg-spinner Clarrie Grimmett bumps into Neville Cardus in Adelaide during the Second World War*

"Only my wife has known what I went through" – *Derbyshire slow left-armer Fred Swarbrook on his chronic yips*

"Poor old googly! It has been subjected to ridicule, abuse, contempt, incredulity – and survived them all" – *Bernard Bosanquet reflects on his famous creation in 1924*

"It was rather a pity Ellis got run out at 1,107 because I was just striking a length" – *New South Wales leg-spinner Arthur Mailey after Victoria's world-record total in 1926*

"I felt like a boy who had killed a dove" – *Mailey after having his hero Victor Trumper stumped third ball in a game of grade cricket*

"You woke up in the night-time and your arm was still going round" – *Left-arm wrist-spinner **Chuck Fleetwood-Smith** after taking 1 for 298 – Test cricket's most expensive analysis – at The Oval in 1938 for Australia against England*

"It's not easy to bat with tears in your eyes" – *Don **Bradman** after finishing his Test career with a second-ball duck at The Oval in 1948, an innings that cost him a career average of 100 by 0.06 of a run*

"I wonder if you see the ball very clearly in your last Test in England on a ground where you've played some of the biggest cricket of your life, and where the opposing team have just stood round you and given you three cheers and the crowd has clapped you all the way to the wicket. I wonder if you really see the ball at all" – ***John Arlott's** commentary*

"That bugger Bradman never had a tear in his eye throughout his whole life" – ***Jack Crapp**, fielding at first slip at the time*

"Thank God Nasser has taken over the Suez Canal. Otherwise, I'd be plastered over every front page like Marilyn Monroe" – *Lancashire groundsman **Bert Flack** after criticism of the Old Trafford pitch on which Jim Laker took 19 wickets in 1956*

"For the first time since I was eight I can go to the beach on a Saturday morning during summer" – *Recently retired Australia seamer **Mike Kasprowicz** suggests life as a professional cricketer may not be all it is cracked up to be*

"I suppose I can take some satisfaction from the fact that my name will be permanently in the record books" – *Glamorgan's **Malcolm Nash**, after being hit for six sixes in an over by Garry Sobers at Swansea in 1968*

"You're the 12th journalist to contact me this week. Yes, I get frustrated. It's been talked about for 40 years. There really is nothing else to add" – *Four decades on, the novelty factor has worn off for **Nash***

"I'm still suffering from flashbacks" – *South Africa's **Herschelle Gibbs** years after dropping Steve Waugh in a crucial World Cup game at Headingley in 1999*

"They're my runs you're clapping. My runs!" – *Geoff Boycott complains to England team-mates, applauding a half-century for Dennis Amiss. Amiss had earlier run Boycott out*

"At the start he'd been applauding Jim's wickets but by the end you could just see him folding his arms" – *England fielder Alan Oakman on Tony Lock at Old Trafford, 1956. Lock took one wicket to Laker's 19*

"I want to play cricket because I have found out that I am rubbish at everything else" – *Australian-turned-Englishman Stuart Law*

"Publicity bothers me. I simply can't see why anyone should be interested in me" – *Somerset opener Mark Lathwell, who briefly played for England in 1993*

"Good luck, the crowd are rooting for you"
"They won't be in a minute when I'm on my way back" – *Lathwell fails to derive confidence from his opening partner Mike Atherton at Headingley against Australia in 1993. Lathwell made a duck*

"Well, I open for Somerset so I may as well go in first" – *Harold Gimblett to fellow sufferers at a mental hospital as they waited for their electroconvulsive therapy*

"Fancy being done by a bloody Chinaman" – *England's Walter Robins after being stumped off Ellis Achong, a Trinidadian of Oriental extraction, at Old Trafford in 1933*

"I bowled one of my best spells in Test cricket and didn't get a wicket – had no luck at all. Both [Ian Botham] came on, bowled a load of rubbish and got a five-for" – *Phil DeFreitas remembers the Melbourne Test of 1986-87*

"He didn't have it all his own way, let me tell you. Well, not for the first couple of overs, anyway" – *Australia leg-spinner Bill O'Reilly remembers the first time he bowled to Don Bradman. By stumps, Bradman was 234 not out*

"Every ball came out of my hand the way I wanted and pitched where I wanted. I beat him twice. It went for 16" – *England leg-spinner Doug Wright on the best over he ever bowled. The batsman was Don Bradman*

CRICKET AND WAR

"Where's the groundsman's hut? If I had a rifle, I'd shoot him now" – *Bill O'Reilly after England's innings-and-579-run win at The Oval in 1938*

"Tougher than commanding a battalion" – *Lieutenant-Colonel John Stephenson on his time as secretary of the MCC*

"They are not going for war, but to play cricket. If somebody is not comfortable, he will not be forced to go. Someone else will go. These are the trusted lieutenants of the country" – *Jagmohan Dalmiya, president of the Indian cricket board, mobilises his troops for Pakistan (and mixes his metaphors) in 2004*

"The worst is when our countries are playing cricket. If they win, we can expect a few gun-shots in celebration, maybe an artillery round or two. If we win, they pound us for hours" – *Indian soldier in Kargil, in the disputed Kashmir region, tells writer Rajiv Rao about the problems cricket can cause for the military*

"There may not be any attacks tonight because we are also watching the match" – *A spokesman for the outlawed Tamil Tigers on halting fighting for Sri Lanka's World Cup semi-final against New Zealand in 2007*

"I have learned a lesson and you will not see me with any more M16s this tournament" – *Ireland batsman Eoin Morgan causes a scare by posing with a security guard's rifle outside a hotel during the World Cup in the Caribbean in 2007*

"It's just a bloody game of cricket and we are in a war" – *Australian umpire Simon Taufel, after the bus carrying match officials – including him – was attacked in Lahore by terrorists*

"I often say to people, 'Yes, I was there.' 'Were you playing?' 'Yes, I got 196'" – *Australia opener Arthur Morris on Bradman's last Test*

"Maybe I'll play for Australia in lawn bowls in the future, maybe tennis, maybe rowing" – *Australia batsman Brad Hodge is fuming after the selectors ignore him*

"I've always said it was handy having my debut Test scores in my surname" – *England opener Graham Gooch, who made a pair against Australia at Edgbaston in 1975*

"A fart competing with thunder" – *Gooch looks back on England's attempts to beat Australia in 1990-91. They lost 3-0*

"It was like a WWF [World Wrestling Federation] punch and I was so shocked that I started crying" – *India seamer Sreesanth after being slapped in the face by Harbhajan Singh following an Indian Premier League match in 2008*

"I was very upset" – *Australia opener Matthew Hayden sheds crocodile tears for Sreesanth*

"I'm afraid I don't know what came over me" – *Middlesex seamer turned broadcaster and journalist Simon Hughes apologises for calling Alec Bedser a 'dobber'*

"I apologised to everyone for my performance" – *Steve Harmison after the first Ashes Test in 2006-07. His opening delivery at Brisbane went straight to second slip*

"Done the elephants, done the poverty. Can we go home now?" – *Tufnell in India, 1992-93*

"I was bowled by an old bugger I thought was dead two thousand years ago, called Robinson Crusoe" – *Essex batsman Charlie McGahey tells his captain how he was dismissed. The bowler, RC Robertson-Glasgow, was known thenceforth as 'Crusoe'*

"It was a mixture of bad bowling, good shots and arse" – *Australia seamer Jason Gillespie on his Ashes series in 2005, when he took three wickets at 100 each*

"Oh, nothing is fine. Just a bit of quiet for a while" – *Kent batsman Ed Smith to team-mate Martin Saggers, who admitted he didn't know what to say after learning Smith had been dropped by England*

"I might have more than 5,000 Test runs, but he makes 40 million bucks a movie" – *New Zealand batsman **Martin Crowe** on his cousin, the Hollywood actor Russell Crowe*

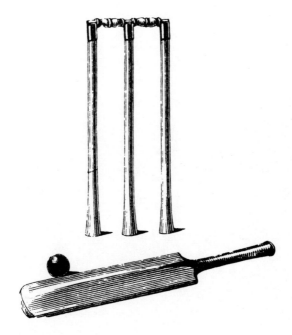

CHAPTER 10

COMPLIMENTS

"He never played a Christian stroke in his life" – *Ted Wainwright, of Yorkshire, on the loose-wristed batting of Ranji*

"He is not a miser hoarding up runs but a millionaire spending them" – *Journalist and author AG Gardiner on Ranji*

"With his wrist held tight Bart could send a new cricket ball to the second storey window with a snip of two fingers and a thumb" – *John A Lester on the manual dexterity of Bart King, America's greatest cricketer*

"He was the Dr Johnson of cricket – as full of his subject, as kindly and as irascible, and just as dogmatic in his dispensations of authority" – *Neville Cardus on WG Grace*

"As near to Bradman as it was possible to get. I never saw anyone play the ball as late as George" – *Len Hutton on George Headley, the West Indies batsman sometimes referred to as the Black Bradman*

"He is a text-book of batting come to life with never a misprint or erratum" – *JM Kilburn, cricket correspondent of the Yorkshire Post, on Don Bradman*

"Come and look at this. You've never seen anything like it" – *Don Bradman calls his team-mates to the Trent Bridge balcony as Stan McCabe goes wild in 1938. He made 232 out of 300 while he was at the wicket*

"If I could play an innings like that I would be a proud man, Stan" – *Bradman afterwards*

"Who does this remind you of?" – *Bradman to his wife Jessie after seeing Sachin Tendulkar on TV for the first time*

"I never saw myself play, but I feel that this player is playing much the same I used to play" – *Bradman on Tendulkar*

"Australia *in excelsis*" – *Neville Cardus on the glamorous all-rounder Keith Miller*

"He could bat, bowl, field and he could fly an aeroplane" – *Bill Brown on his Australia colleague Miller*

"Whenever Ken walked to the wicket I thought a Union Jack was trailing behind him" – *Australia wicketkeeper **Wally Grout** on England batsman Ken Barrington*

"On his day he has displayed, to the highest degree, the beauty and skill and the manliness and the terror of his calling" – *Cricket journalist **John Woodcock** on Fred Trueman*

"Surely no one among his contemporaries with such a statistical record has played so many crooked strokes" – *John Arlott on Hampshire captain Colin Ingleby-Mackenzie*

"He could charm even the enemy" – *Hampshire wicket-keeper **Leo Harrison** on Ingleby-Mackenzie*

"We applauded him all the way, for here was a man who could steal a West Indian heart" – ***Garry Sobers** on Colin Milburn's 94 at Old Trafford in 1966*

"The bank clerk who went to war" – ***Clive Taylor** of the Sun on an unlikely hero, the grey-haired, bespectacled England batsman David Steele in 1975*

"You could have put a pint of bitter on his head and he wouldn't have spilled a drop" – ***Tom Cartwright** admires Viv Richards' stillness at the crease*

"You're a couple of bandits, but you can play" – ***Bill Lawry**, captain of Australia, to the Chappell brothers, Ian and Greg*

"Valour was the better part of discretion" – *Australian writer **Warwick Franks** on dashing batsman David Hookes*

"The face of a choirboy, the demeanour of a civil servant and the ruthlessness of a rat-catcher" – *Geoff Boycott on England left-arm spinner Derek Underwood*

"I know you. You are the Destroyer" – *Nelson Mandela meets England fast bowler Devon Malcolm in 1995-96, not long after he had taken 9 for 57 against South Africa at The Oval*

"Where is Brian Lara?" – *Mandela arrives in Trinidad*

"I used to call him 'Mr Gooch'" – *Shane Warne reveals a rare degree of respect for an English batsman*

"He was so good it was sometimes embarrassing to bat at the other end" – *Steve Waugh on Matthew Hayden*

"I found him a decent person, unlike normal cricketers" – *Pakistan's Wasim Bari on India's Rahul Dravid*

"Sachin Tendulkar is, in my time, the best player without doubt. Daylight second, Brian Lara third" – *Warne*

"You know genius when you see it. And let me tell you, Sachin is pure genius" – *Brian Lara*

"I suppose I can say 'I was there' at the moment he first indicated his potential to the wider world. There or thereabouts anyway" – *England batsman Mike Gatting after being bowled by Warne at Old Trafford in 1993*

"Sometimes when I bat, even now, when I feel a little loose, I think about him" – *Sourav Ganguly on the rather more nuggety Steve Waugh*

"That's the overriding positive feeling about having retired from international cricket – not having that big bugger charging in at me" – *Australia opener Justin Langer won't miss facing Andrew Flintoff*

"We've got to get this guy to South Africa" – *England coach Duncan Fletcher to Michael Vaughan after watching Pietersen's first two one-day internationals, in Zimbabwe. Once in South Africa, he averaged over 150 in a losing cause*

"I couldn't have played that shot and I'm left-handed" – *David Gower on Pietersen's switch-hit*

"I was drinking my cup of tea and spat it out. We were watching live and then all ran into the dressing-room to watch it on the telly because we were not actually sure we'd just seen that" – *England all-rounder Stuart Broad on the reaction to Pietersen's switch-hit*

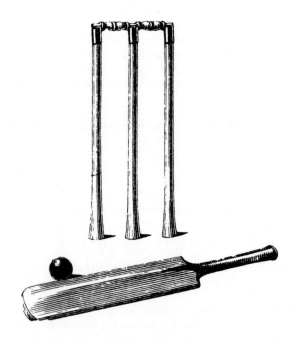

CHAPTER 11

NON-PLAYERS

"I'm a little stiff from bowling"
"Oh, is that where you're from. I was wondering" – *Unnamed princess to Australia leg-spinner Arthur Mailey in the royal box at Lord's in 1921*

"If you don't take the job, you're fired" – *Freddie Brown's boss at a firm of engineers responds to Brown's request for leave to captain England in Australia in 1950-51*

"I've been watching that Lawry all day down at The Oval. I'm in no mood to put up with any more bloody nonsense" – *A taxi driver ferrying Jack Fingleton and Neville Cardus through Soho after knocking out a man who had tapped his cab after it became stuck in a crowd*

"You have done for Australian cricket what the Boston Strangler did for door-to-door salesmen" – *Jack Birney, an Australian politician, drops Geoff Boycott a note after he batted all day in a Test in Perth for 63*

"Sachin was so focused. He never looked like getting out. He was batting with single-minded devotion. It was truly remarkable. It was a lesson" – *Tennis star Martina Navratilova joins the Sachin Tendulkar fan club after watching him bat at Sydney in 2003-04*

"I'm not a big cricket man myself, but even I found myself watching it, watching how tense it was, down to the last ball" – *David Beckham after Australia hang on nine down to draw the Old Trafford Test of 2005*

"I must say, I'm very impressed with that Mr Pietersen. His life story is like Henry IV, V and VI all rolled into one" – *Bruce Dickinson, former lead singer of Iron Maiden*

"When some of these people hear it's in African countries, some of them think we are monkeys out there in the rainforest" – *Kingori Mwangi, a spokesman for the Kenyan police, reacts to New Zealand's decision not to play in his country at the 2003 World Cup*

"He had his fists clenched in the air and was roaring at the top of his voice like a wild animal. Thank God the ball hit the railing. Someone could have been killed" – *Eyewitness* **John Selby** *cowers in terror after Mark Vermeulen, the former Zimbabwe international, goes berserk during a Central Lancashire League match for Werneth against Ashton. Vermeulen had responded to taunts from the crowd by hurling a ball in their direction and was subsequently banned from all cricket in England and Wales for ten years. The ban was later reduced to three years – the second and third suspended – after an appeal*

"I told my mate that was Knotty and Denness – we'll stop them and ask them what happened at Headingley" – *A policeman tells* **Mike Denness**, *driving home with Alan Knott rather too quickly after the 1975 World Cup semi-final defeat to Australia, why he pulled them over*

"I'm not Bradman, I'm 'Utton'" – **Hugh Hunter**, *a letter writer to* The Times, *reveals the response of a small boy batting in the street to whom he had shouted out "Hello Bradman". Three days before the letter is published, in 1938, Hutton made 364 at The Oval, passing Bradman's Test record*

"The effect was as though a particularly grumpy taxi-driver had started quoting Dr Johnson while sorting out your change" – *Dave Gelly in the* Observer *on the cricket-loving auto-didact Benny Green*

"You know the cricket season has arrived when you hear the sound of leather on Brian Close" – *Comedian* **Eric Morecambe**

"Be content with a cellar of wine and the society of those who love you" – *The poet* **Hilaire Belloc** *to his old university friend, CB Fry, after Fry was offered the throne of Albania*

"Tell me, Mr Ferguson, do you use an adding machine when the Don comes to bat?" – *George VI to Australia's team scorer at Balmoral in 1948*

"Mark Taylor, the Australian captain? Ah, but for how long" – *Customs official to Mark Taylor upon arrival in England in 1997*

"The sound of his bat somehow puts me in mind of vintage port" – *AA Milne of Jack Hobbs*

"That's the weirdest David Gower I've ever seen" – *Antony Costa, a member of pop group Blue, reveals rhyming slang for 'shower' on the reality television show* I'm a Celebrity, Get Me Out of Here!

"Team sports like cricket should not be included in the Olympics. Olympics is a personal game where a sportsman tries to excel within himself" – *100m Olympic gold medallist Linford Christie*

"As I watch the ball soar high over the turf, it comes to me in a flash that I should leave The Stranglers tonight, after the gig" – *Hugh Cornwell, lead singer, explains his decision to leave his band after watching Devon Malcolm hit a six against India at Old Trafford in 1990*

"Had he been playing in this day and age there would not have been an unsponsored inch of him" – *Writer and broadcaster Michael Parkinson on Denis Compton*

"Are you aware, sir, that the last time I saw anything like that on a top lip, the whole herd had to be destroyed?" – *Eric Morecambe to Dennis Lillee*

"Before you bank it, take it to the other pub and show it to the bloke who wouldn't give us any food" – *Kerry Packer, after handing over a cheque to a pub landlord for £100,128 for a £128 spread of late-night ham sandwiches*

CRICKET AND THE THEATRE

"Cricket is first and foremost a dramatic spectacle. It belongs with the theatre, ballet, opera and the dance" – *Historian CLR James*

"Of course it's frightfully dull! That's the whole point!" – *Robert Morley's character in* The Final Test, *filmed in 1953*

CRICKET AND THE THEATRE

"This is like dying and going to heaven" – *Actor Boris Karloff on the Lord's balcony*

"I have often thought of how much better a life I would have had, what a better man I would have been, how much healthier an existence I would have led, had I been a cricketer" – *Sir Laurence Olivier*

"It's better than getting an Oscar. I think I must be the only actor ever to have been an honorary member, and certainly the only socialist" – *Alan Curtis after being made an honorary member of the MCC*

"I'd also like to thank Denis Compton, a boyhood hero of mine" – *Tim Rice after winning an Oscar in 1995 for Best Original Song (from* The Lion King*)*

"We don't know who Denis Compton is. He doesn't appear to be at Disney Studios or have anything to do with *The Lion King*" – *Bemused spokesman for the Academy of Motion Picture Arts and Sciences*

"He came into the dressing room holding a cigarette holder, wearing a dressing gown, sandals and a T-shirt with a picture of Darren Gough on it" – *Actor Sean Bean meets Peter O'Toole*

"Tom was so moved he was practically in tears. He enjoyed it so much he hired the box himself for a match the next day" – *Director Sam Mendes after taking Tom Cruise to the SCG for a one-day international and explaining how Mark Taylor had once declared on 334 not out to avoid overtaking Don Bradman's career-best*

"The instant, one-day game is rather like a one-act play, whereas a five-day Test corresponds to Elizabethan five-act drama with its swift reversals of fortune and cumulative tension" – *Theatre critic Michael Billington*

CHAPTER 12

THEY ALSO SERVE...

"Cricket is not a circus and it would be far better that it should be driven back to the village green than yield a jot to the petulant demands of the spectator" – **Pelham Warner**, *English cricket grandee, did not believe the customer was king*

"Here, give me your autograph book and I'll sign it"
"I ain't got one"
"Then what do you want?"
"Please, sir, you're the only decent bit of shade in the place" – *Conversation between* **Warwick Armstrong**, *well-proportioned captain of Australia, and a* **young boy** *at Southampton in 1921*

"Blimey, what are you worrying about? It's only a quarter of a thousand" – *A wag in the crowd puts the moment Bradman reached 250 at Lord's in 1930 into perspective*

"It's all very well for you to tell me to snap out of it. I know it's only a game but there are millions of cricket-lovers back in England in the middle of floods and gales and blizzards and this is a nice thing to happen to them, isn't it?" – *England captain* **Len Hutton** *responds to a well-wisher after losing the opening Ashes Test in 1954-55 by an innings and 154 having stuck Australia in*

"Come on lightning, strike twice" – **Heckler** *to Australia opener Bill Lawry during an Ashes rearguard at Sydney in 1962-63. Lawry had just hit a rare boundary*

"Harvey and Davidson are quitting the game, but they shouldn't be lonely as they are retiring at the same time as 100,000 spectators" – *A* **Sydney journalist** *bemoans the drab cricket that series*

"A cricket tour in Australia would be the most delightful period in your life – if you were deaf" – *England's Bodyline pack-leader* **Harold Larwood**

"Leave our flies alone, Jardine! They're the only flamin' friends you've got here" – *Another earful for England's Bodyline captain, Douglas Jardine*

"Come on, Eddie, give it to this bastard. It was his bloody forefathers who took all that land from your bloody forefathers" – *Brisbane spectator to Eddie Gilbert, very fast Aboriginal bowler, bowling to Jardine*

"You've spoilt my weekend. I could hit you. Why did you bowl out Don Bradman for a duck?" – *Small boy to England seamer Alec Bedser in Glenelg near Adelaide in 1946-47*

"Unless action is taken swiftly I fear a cricketer will be killed before too long" – *England's* **Mike Brearley** *following crowd abuse in Sydney*

"It's common to be followed round the ground with kids shouting 'Pommie bastards'. Some of the stones they throw aren't small either" – *England seamer* **Graham Dilley**, *on tour Down Under*

"Hey, Willis! I didn't know they stacked crap that high" – *Australian fan to England fast bowler Bob Willis*

"Hey, Underwood! You're so slow you can read the adverts while you're running after the bloody ball" – *Australian fan to England spinner Derek Underwood*

"I remember when someone asked me for my autograph and when I went over they slapped a minced beef and onion pie on my head" – *England's* **Phil Tufnell** *enjoys his banter with the Australians*

"Tufnell, can I borrow your brain? I'm building an idiot" – *Barracker to Tufnell*

"I can't repeat what the Australian fans said. I thought I was a reasonable bloke until yesterday" – *England and Lancashire batsman* **Mal Loye** *experiences international cricket for the first time*

"It is hard in Australia when you are losing. Even the kids in the street start smirking when they see you and then you hear them giggling behind your back. We could do with putting a stop to all that" – *Michael Vaughan*

"Funnily enough, the younger they are, the nastier stuff they say. I didn't know six-year-old kids could swear like that" – *South Africa spinner Paul Harris is exposed to the crowds in Australia*

"I don't mind when people boo me. The more they do it, the more I'm going to play hard. Actually, it gives me pleasure that everyone knows me at the ground. It inspires me to do well" – *Indian spinner Harbhajan Singh just loves Australian crowds*

"Those people belong to the jungle and the forest instead of a civilized country" – *India opener Sunil Gavaskar on the baying Jamaican crowd*

"I looked straight at him. He pulled out a magnum, pointed it at me and pulled the trigger. I froze. Obviously it wasn't loaded or I wouldn't be here to tell the tale" – *Australia seamer Paul Reiffel on tour in South Africa in 1996-97*

"If this letter reaches you, the Post Office thinks more of you than I do" – *Letter to England captain Mike Denness after the 1974-75 tour of Australia*

"He's over here, disguised in dreadlocks" – *West Indies fans to Jonathan Agnew, hopeful the chairman of selectors Peter May was watching his efforts for Leicestershire in a tour game in 1988*

"Waugh! What is he good for? Absolutely nothing" – *England fans' chant to Steve Waugh in 1993, with apologies to Edwin Starr*

"Worthy souls dwell among them no doubt. As a group, they too often demean English cricket. As Betjeman prayed of Slough: come friendly bombs and fall on them. Water bombs will do" – *Christopher Martin-Jenkins on the Barmy Army*

"These people stand behind a fence drinking beer with most of them 50 kilos overweight making ridiculous comments" – *Australia opener* **Justin Langer** *after the Barmy Army greet every delivery from fast bowler Brett Lee with a cry of "no-ball"*

"I was calling him 'potato' in Punjabi because he is a little fat" – *Spectator taunts Inzamam-ul-Haq during a game in Toronto. Inzamam responded by wading into the crowd with a bat, and was banned for two matches*

"What's wrong with the offer? I know several people who are living without a kidney" – **Sarun Sharma**, *an Indian fan, offers to sell a body part for £3,500 to pay his way to the 2007 World Cup in the Caribbean*

"If I was sitting in an armchair then I'd be disappointed as well" – *India captain* **Rahul Dravid** *responds to the armchair fans who criticised him for not asking England to follow on at The Oval in 2007*

"OK, so I might not be the real Mohammad Yousuf, but I have a valid ticket and I have every right to watch the match" – **Mohammad Shafiq**, *a Mohammad Yousuf lookalike, after trying to gain access to the Pakistan dressing room*

"Shane, I think I'm pregnant" – **Banner** *at the Adelaide Oval during the 2006-07 Ashes*

"Yes WI can" – *A* **placard** *at Sabina Park as England are skittled for 51 in February 2009*

CHAPTER 13

UMPIRES

"What are the butchers for?" – *American actress **Pauline Chase** spies the men in white coats at her first cricket match*

"It is one of the misapprehensions of cricket. Umpires are assumed to be merry inkeeper types, Falstaffian figures, whereas they have as many anxieties as the rest of us" – Wisden *editor **Scyld Berry***

"If anyone were to ask us the question 'what class of useful men receive most abuse and least thanks for their service?' we should, without hesitation, reply, 'Cricket umpires'" – ***AG Steel** in* The Badminton Library – Cricket

"It is not cricket to keep asking the umpire" – ***John Lillywhite's** Cricketers' Companion in 1867*

"Sorry, Jim. My foot slipped"
"Sorry Spoff. My tongue slipped" – *Conversation between Australia fast bowler **Fred Spofforth**, who had just bowled a no-ball, and umpire **Jim Phillips**, who proceeded to call the next delivery, a legitimate one, a no-ball too*

"You no-ball my good balls and the ones I did throw, you never. You know nothing about cricket" – *Aborigine fast bowler **Albert 'Alec' Henry** to a Brisbane umpire*

"Just thought you might make two mistakes in one day" – *South Australia left-arm seamer **Bill Whitty** appeals for a non-existent catch after the umpire had turned down a good shout for caught behind*

"You're out and we've won" – *Welsh umpire **Dai Davies** gives out Hampshire's Charlie Knott to seal Glamorgan's first championship title, in 1948*

"Doubt? When I'm umpiring there's never any doubt" – *English umpire* **Frank Chester**

"Three kicks and yer out" – *Australian umpire Cec Pepper's habitual warning to batsmen who liked to use their pads*

"I used to shoot 'em out, no matter who" – *Pepper refused to do captains any favours*

"You hold it, mate, and use it as a pisspot" – *Pepper to Dennis Amiss, who had asked him to hold his helmet*

"Not out, you fat Australian bastard" – *League umpire to Pepper during his playing days, when his own language wasn't exactly squeaky clean either*

"One friend said Cec was the only man he knew who could talk, spit, chew, belch and pass wind simultaneously" – Wisden *obituary on Pepper in 1994*

"I am finished. I can no longer see the ball" – *Glamorgan opener* **Emrys Davies** *decides to call it a day in 1954 ... at which point he became a first-class umpire, standing in nine Tests*

"I can't see without 'em and on hot days I can't see with 'em, because they get steamed up. So I bowl on hearing only and appeal twice an over" – *Bespectacled bowler* **Alex Skelding**, *who went on to become an umpire*

"I hope you don't mind me mentioning this but you're the worst bowler I've ever seen" – **Arthur Jepson** *to Lancashire's occasional slow left-armer David Lloyd*

"Christ, how does he do it? He's only got to miss it and he'll be lbw" – *English umpire to Somerset's Peter Robinson on Viv Richards' ability to work straight balls through the leg-side*

"Those weren't bouncers. Over here we call them long hops" – *West Indian umpire to England's Keith Fletcher after he was greeted by five successive short balls at Trinidad in 1973-74*

"For treatment. He thinks that last ball may have broken his finger" – *Indian umpire to England bowler John Price in 1963-64 after Price, convinced he had the batsman caught off the glove, asked why he was leaving the field having been given not out*

"Hit the ball and I'm given out lbw. Missed it and I'm given out caught. I've no excuses" – *England opener* **Tim Robinson** *on tour in India in 1984-85*

"I'm sorry, Mr Brearley. I knew it wasn't out. But my hand started moving upwards and I couldn't do anything to stop it" – *Indian umpire apologises to England's Mike Brearley after wrongly giving him out on a tour match*

"I was infuriated by the injustice of it all. [Rex] Whitehead had stood in all three Tests and many bad decisions by him have gone against us" – *India opener* **Sunil Gavaskar** *after trying to lead his opening partner Chetan Chauhan off the field following his dismissal to Dennis Lillee at Melbourne in February 1981*

"He spat the dummy right out of the pram" – *Lillee's take on the incident*

"We couldn't let the f**kers get away with it" – **Unnamed English official** *after Pakistan's request for umpire David Constant not to stand in their Tests on their 1987 tour was ignored*

"Not that silly trick again" – **Shakoor Rana** *after Sussex's John Barclay tried to persuade the Pakistani umpire to lift his finger to the skies by shouting, "Where's Allah?"*

"You are a f**king cheating c**t" – **Rana** *accuses England captain Mike Gatting of moving fielders behind the batsman's back at Faisalabad in 1987*

"When it does, once every ten years or so, it really goes" – **Gatting** *on his temper*

"I apologise for the bad language used during the second Test at Fisalabad [sic]" – **Gatting** *begrudgingly tries to smooth things over with a brief note to Rana*

"Oh God, not you again" – *Gatting bumps into Rana in England after a tabloid paper paid for the umpire to try to shake his hand for the benefit of a photographer. Gatting simply drove off*

"And that, gentlemen, is the end of another f**king over" – *Unnamed umpire returns sweater to Australian fast bowler Merv Hughes at the end of an expletive-laden over in a game against Nottinghamshire in 1989*

"Count 'em yourself, you Pommie c**t" – *Australian umpire* **Peter McConnell***'s alleged reply to Phil Tufnell after he had been asked how many balls were left in the over at Melbourne in 1990-91*

"I would defend the English umpires against charges of intentional bias, but I would not be completely sure that there is no trace of subliminal prejudice" – *England's* **Mike Brearley** *as Pakistan's tourists fume about English officialdom in 1992*

"If we appeared to have batted in a hurry, it is because the batsmen want to make the most of their short stay before the umpires do them in" – ***Bandula Warnapura****, manager of the Sri Lankan tourists in India in 1993-94. Sri Lanka lost the Test series 3-0*

"I wonder if bowlers who are verbally happy to chirp at umpires with such cracks as 'Are you blind?', 'How could you make that decision?', would enjoy it if umpires, after a bad ball, said things such as 'Call yourself a Test bowler?', 'Hell, my grandson is more accurate than you' or 'What a lot of rubbish, how on earth did you get into the Test side?' – *Australia captain* **Bob Simpson**

"I'm in charge of this game. You'll stand where I want you to. If you don't stand there, there won't be a game" – *Sri Lanka captain* **Arjuna Ranatunga** *bosses around the Australian umpire Ross Emerson after Emerson called Muttiah Muralitharan for chucking in a one-day game against England at Adelaide*

"Give me Simon Taufel and Aleem Dar any day. Billy Bowden's a show pony, Steve Bucknor is well past his sell-by date, and Daryl Harper's just hopeless" – *Bob Willis on the more recent breed of umpires*

CRICKET AND THE LAW

"All I was doing was holding it" – *Chris Hurd, a 28-year-old accountant and occasional leg-spinner, questioned by police for 10 minutes after being caught in possession of a cricket ball on the London Underground*

"It's an invasion of human rights" – *Father of Carl Ferris, a Yeovil schoolboy, who was banned from classes after sporting a spiky haircut à la Kevin Pietersen*

"I'm sorry, I was going too fast in your country. I love playing cricket in England" – *Shane Warne in a letter to Ilkeston magistrates after being caught doing 120mph on the M1 in Derbyshire*

"I'd rather face Dennis Lillee with a stick of rhubarb than go through that again" – *Ian Botham after being acquitted of assault after a fracas in a Scunthorpe nightclub*

"You could hit blokes in the head in those days and after the game have a drink with them. These days, you could end up in court" – *Rodney Hogg, full-on Australia fast bowler, on the danger of the modern beamer*

"He is my third umpire" – *New Zealand umpire Billy Bowden on God*

"He's got to be given his pension book. He is hopeless" – *Willis repeats his views on Harper after his controversial application of the new referral system in the West Indies-England series in 2008-09*

"That Billy Bowden, what a twerp" – *Geoff Boycott after Bowden refers a catch claimed by Boycott's fellow Yorkshire player Michael Vaughan in a Test at Headingley*

"Let's hope the Bangladeshis go as long as their national anthem" – *Simon Taufel ahead of Australia v Bangladesh at Darwin in 2003. Taufel later apologised*

"Andre unfortunately only had one line that he was dishing out to Shoaib Malik and the boys so it got a bit monotonous there. We just had a chat to Andre and said to Graeme Smith, 'Well, look he's only traipsing out one line, it's getting a bit boring'" – *Taufel loses patience with the repetitiveness of South Africa seamer Andre Nel's sledging*

"A most unfortunate precedent, however, has now been established. Any umpire who in future makes a decision which angers one of the Asian Test-playing countries – India, Pakistan, Sri Lanka and Bangladesh – can expect the wrath of the Asian bloc to descend upon his head" – *Scyld Berry on the ICC's decision to remove Darrell Hair from their panel of elite umpires after he accused Pakistan of tampering with the ball at The Oval in 2006*

"Because I'm pretty bloody good at it" – *Hair explains why he wasn't retiring*

"I feel devastated and let down by the ICC. Since the final Test at The Oval, no one from ICC has shown any concern for my welfare or for the welfare of my family. My family has suffered the pain of reading headlines such as 'disgraced former umpire' and 'sacked former umpire' and I have found it difficult to cope with daily life in the knowledge that I have not been given a reasonable opportunity to defend myself or make a representation to the board in person" – *Hair explains his state of mind at a tribunal in London where he briefly pursued a claim of racial discrimination against the ICC*

"I thought it was a bit rude when the umpire gestured me with a finger so I showed my middle one back" – *Crystal Palace FC's Finnish midfielder Aki Riihilahti plays cricket for the first time*

"Don't you lecture me, it was an arsehole decision" – *Geoff Boycott to third umpire Asad Rauf following a controversial run-out decision in a Pakistan-England Test*

"Players are not generally the best judges. That's why we have umpires" – *Mike Atherton on the referral system*

"There is a popular misconception that umpires are a refuge of time-warp-locked geriatrics waiting for a listing in Genesis" – *Barrie Stuart-King, chairman of the Association of Cricket Umpires and Scorers, stands up for his members*

"I cannot for the life of me see why the umpires, the only two people on a cricket field who are not going to get grass stains on their knees, are the only two people allowed to wear dark trousers" – *British journalist Katharine Whitehorn*

"It's similar to the situation where you are sitting at home and the answer to a quiz question on TV looks very simple but you just lose your train of thought when you are in that heated pressure situation" – *ICC's general manager Dave Richardson after his elite five-man team of match officials misinterprets the Duckworth/Lewis method in the 2007 World Cup final*

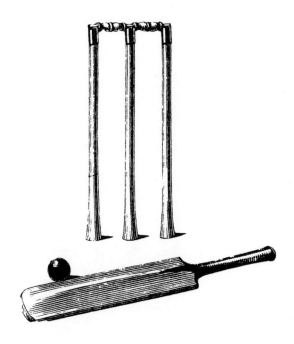

CHAPTER 14

COACHES

"A coach who suppresses natural instincts may find that he has lifted a poor player to a mediocre one but has reduced a potential genius to the rank and file" – *Don Bradman*

"When you see a cricket coach, run off as fast as you can" – *Australia leg-spinner Bill O'Reilly*

"We flippin' murdered 'em" – *England coach David Lloyd after Zimbabwe escape with a draw with the scores level against England at Bulawayo in 1996-97*

"His hero ducks into a short one so what does he do? He goes and sobs over him like a girl guide" – *South Africa's Ray Jennings after Andre Nel fells Allan Donald in a South African domestic game*

"If England fire a rifle, I want to fire a cannon. If they fire a peashooter, I want us to be firing a bazooka" – *Jennings, later appointed South Africa's coach, reveals the way he plans to tackle Steve Harmison in 2004-05*

"If the players expect soft drinks, I will make sure there are none. They will go to a tap and get on their knees and drink water until they realise that it is an honour to play for South Africa" – *Jennings lays down the rules for the team shortly after taking over*

"Jennings was to orthodoxy what King Herod was to child-minding" – *Mike Atherton*

"It is one thing having a hard nut as a coach, quite another having simply a nut" – *Journalist Neil Manthorp on Jennings*

"It hit me. Suddenly at that moment the magnitude of this day must have come crashing into my body. I began retching" – *England's* **Duncan Fletcher** *reveals the extent of his nerves ahead of the last day of the 2005 Ashes*

"I've always said the coach is something you should go to the ground in" – **Shane Warne** *on numerous occasions*

"He has been known to have us work on our juggling, as though we were about to join a circus" – **Warne** *on Australia coach John Buchanan*

"We had to listen to his verbal diarrhoea all the time. He is just a goose and has no idea and lacks common sense" – **Warne** *on Buchanan again*

"John must have misunderstood what I was saying. He must have been listening to something else, his computer, or something" – **Warne** *responds to claims that Buchanan thought he might be reconsidering a return to one-day international cricket*

"It was a waste of time. The boot camp was a different way to reinforce the same things. My way would have been to lock us all up in a pub" – **Warne** *on Buchanan's novel method of forging team spirit ahead of the 2006-07 Ashes*

"How could he be so vain, so stupid, so self-centred to forget about the team? Why did he think he was bullet-proof?" – **Buchanan** *hits out in his autobiography at Warne's one-year drugs ban in 2003*

"I finished the Ashes physically and emotionally drained. Looking back, I ought not to have retreated into myself the way I did" – **Buchanan** *admits his mistakes in 2005*

"I love each and every one of you but, like my own family, you thrill, you frustrate, you anger" – **Buchanan** *in a letter to Australia's players after they lose to India at Adelaide in 2005-06*

"The batting efforts of our opposition are not assisting the development of our bowlers' one-day skills" – **Buchanan** *after England are bowled out for 110 at Adelaide. He should have been careful what he wished for: Australia lost their next three games to the English*

"I always find it funny when a team feels it has to go out there and defend itself against talk that they are mentally scarred. From my experience, if you don't bring things up, you're probably not worried about them. But if you feel the need to go out there and make all sorts of statements and denials, then you probably are in a bit of trouble" – *Buchanan's replacement, Tim Nielsen, gets stuck into South Africa following their World Cup semi-final defeat to Australia in 2007*

"I told them at the interval we had a chance, but I didn't really believe it. I only said it to keep their spirits up" – *Mansoor Rana, the coach of Pakistan Under-19s, after his side won the 2005-06 World Cup defending only 109 against India in the final*

"This is do or die. I will put myself in the Atlantic if we lose" – *Taj Malik Alam of Afghanistan is keen for his side to qualify for the 2011 World Cup. He was later sacked*

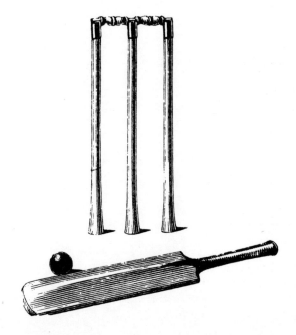

CHAPTER 15

FAMILY AFFAIRS

"Well I never, it's those two again" – *The wife of Sir Robert Menzies, prime minister of Australia, after turning up to Lord's in 1926 and seeing Jack Hobbs and Herbert Sutcliffe walk out to bat. On her only previous trip to a Test match, at Melbourne in 1925, the pair had batted all day. And by the time the Menzies' left Lord's just before tea, they were still batting*

"Given her views throughout the affair, it would have been easy for Brenda to say, 'I told you so', but instead all she did was to look as upset as I felt" – *Graham Gooch on his wife after he was banned from Test cricket for three years for taking part in a rebel tour to South Africa*

"I'll get my wife to do it next time" – *Australia's **Brad Hogg** makes a hash of trimming his finger-nails. One becomes infected, briefly putting him at risk of missing a one-day series against New Zealand*

"I don't ask my wife to face Michael Holding, so there's no reason why I should be changing nappies" – *Ian Botham leaves Kath out of the equation*

"She probably cost me a century. I went into my shell for a while after that" – *Club cricketer **Clive Scott** after hitting his wife Sharon on the head with a six while she was pushing their baby round the boundary edge*

"He's got a reputation for being awkward and arrogant, probably because he is awkward and arrogant" – *Frances Edmonds on her husband, the Middlesex and England left-arm spinner Phil*

"So, you're the guy who nearly killed my husband" – *Frances meets West Indies (very) fast bowler Patrick Patterson on tour with England in 1985-86*

"I genuinely do ask myself why I am wandering around the Caribbean in solitary confinement, made to feel awkward and marginalised by a combination of resentful, suspicious, unsympathetic, guilty-conscience-ridden, socially inadequate, educational sub-to-more-or-less-normal cricketers" – *Edmonds again*

"Cricketers rarely get too animated. I'm no different. When my wife presented me with our first child, the best I could manage in the delivery room was 'err ... well done'. It's the cricketer in me. You always stay underwhelmed" – *Australia leg-spinner* **Kerry O'Keeffe**

"It's much better than being a footballer – in that game half the nation hates you because you play for the wrong club. That must be hell" – *Rachael Flintoff, wife of Andrew, is delighted her husband chose cricket*

"I did call him Freddie once, but he said: 'No, you can't call me Freddie. I'm Andrew to you'" – *Rachael gets used to being married to a national hero*

"I had to ask if he was a batter or a bowler – I didn't really know who he was" – *Liberty X singer* **Jessica Taylor** *on fiancé Pietersen*

"He said I had a 'nice-looking ass' and asked me for my number. I gave it to him" – *Helen Cohen Alon, from Johannesburg, alleges sexual harassment against Shane Warne*

"Those rumours are complete horse manure. We've been together seven years and we're happier than ever" – *Sir Allen Stanford reacts to speculation that his fiancée – and employee – Andrea Stoelker was fired because of a liaison with West Indies captain Chris Gayle*

"He's a boy you could take home to your mother" – *TV presenter* **Anne Robinson** *on England all-rounder Paul Collingwood*

"We're getting guys dragging their girlfriends to the theatre, which is the opposite of how it usually works" – *Eddie Perfect, the lead in* Shane Warne – The Musical

"Heredity, except in very rare instances, goes for nothing in Test cricket. You are just as likely to make a century or take five wickets against Australia if your father is an engine-driver, an average-adjuster, a novelist, and a cricketphobe" – *RC Robertson-Glasgow*

"If I get hit, Dad, stop Mum from jumping the fence" – *Australia's* **Stan McCabe**, *aged 22, prepares to bat at Sydney during the Bodyline series*

"We are, for all purposes, one" – **Eric Bedser** *on his relationship with his twin brother Alec*

"That'll be Dad" – **Don Bradman**'s *son, John, reacts to the roar from the stand as he leaves the Adelaide Oval on the evening Alec Bedser bowled the Don for a duck in 1946-47*

"She improved my love of vegetables by introducing the phrase 'you can't go out and play cricket until you have eaten all your vegetables'" – **Richie Benaud** *on his mother, who lived to the age of 104*

"Dear, a lot of commentators are saying you should give up hooking. Maybe you should consider it" – *Ian Chappell's gran,* **Dorothy**, *in an aerogramme during the 1972 Ashes*

"I have to get this off my chest. Do you think you should have hit over the top so early?" – *Dermot Reeve's mother,* **Monica**, *after he had fallen in a county game to Ray Illingworth*

"Why did you get out to such a silly shot?" – **Anjali Tendulkar** *tells off her husband*

"Even my father's name is Sachin Tendulkar" – *His daughter,* **Sara**, *after her schoolteacher tells the class there is a restaurant in Mumbai named after him*

"I suppose me mum'll speak to me. Reckon me dad will too. And my wife. But who else?" – **Kim Hughes**, *captain of Australia when they lost to England at Headingley in 1981 after enforcing the follow-on*

"My wife had an uncle who could never walk down the nave of an abbey without wondering whether it would take spin" – *British Prime Minister Sir Alec Douglas-Home, whose ten-match first-class career spanned six different teams*

"Oh, congratulations. But you've got my husband's job" – *Michelle Marsh, wife of Geoff, to Mark Taylor, who had just replaced him as Australia's vice-captain*

"Pakistan is the sort of place every man should send his mother-in-law to, for a month, all expenses paid" – *Ian Botham returns home after England lose 1-0 in Pakistan in 1983-84*

"Why don't you send in your mother-in-law now? She couldn't do any worse" – *Pakistan's Aamir Sohail waits eight years for revenge after Botham's duck in the 1992 World Cup final*

"I think he would have got a hundred just hitting along the ground. The next bloody thing that comes out is that sweep and, jeez, I hate that shot" – *Rodger Waugh, Steve's father, reflects on his son's final Test innings: caught on the boundary slog-sweeping for 80*

"Read it? She'd run down the pitch before he'd bowl it. She'd be working in the kitchen with her pinny on and smack it!" – *Geoff Boycott explains what his mum would do to the googly of West Indies leg-spinner Rawl Lewis*

"Yes, I am Mrs Hoggard. And I've been listening to your crap for the last hour. My husband's made you look a right tit" – *Matthew Hoggard's wife, Sarah, to TV personality Piers Morgan after Morgan had bad-mouthed her husband within earshot during the Trent Bridge Ashes Test in 2005. Hoggard proceeded to take three quick wickets to turn the game*

"I'm glad I didn't catch it now because he would have laughed so much that it would have been the end of his innings" – *Colin Flintoff, Andrew's dad, after dropping a catch off his son in the stands at Edgbaston*

"At night I'd lie there and go, 'S**t, when am I going to see my kids?' There were times I'd sit there and drink my mini bar until three in the morning just to get to sleep... I cried a fair bit when I was by myself'" – *Shane Warne on tour in England in 2005 after his divorce*

THE LADIES

"Given the choice between Raquel Welch and a hundred at Lord's, I'd take the hundred every time" – *Geoff Boycott. Welch's son married the daughter of Fred Trueman, a Yorkshire colleague of Boycott*

"The truth is Elle Macpherson could have been standing in front of me naked as the day she was born and I wouldn't have noticed" – *Phil Tufnell, who supposedly snubbed his captain Graham Gooch's outstretched hand after taking his first Test wicket*

"Ladies playing cricket? Absurd. Just like a man trying to knit" – *More old-school Yorkshire open-mindedness, this time from* **Len Hutton**

"Tell you what, Michael. I won't tell you how to fockin' bat and you don't tell me how to fockin' cook. All right?" – *Nancy Doyle, fearsome former head of the Middlesex kitchen, responds to Mike Brearley's request for "something a little less substantial"*

"I really can't see any great advantage in having women in the pavilion. In fact, I can see some disadvantages" – *John Stephenson, MCC secretary, in 1991. Women were finally admitted to the club in 1999*

"Over half the audience is female and they don't want technical cricket stuff, they want the sound of a comforting voice while they're doing the housework, or whatever they're doing" – *Henry Blofeld tells* Wisden Cricket Monthly *how the BBC's* Test Match Special *has kept up with the times*

"There is no significant difference in how men and women play cricket, nor in the way it is administered" – *Maria Grant at the tribunal which awarded her £15,000 compensation after she failed to make the shortlist for the role of assistant secretary of the Lancashire Cricket Board. She was told she lacked knowledge of men's cricket*

THE LADIES

"It's kind of hard to go on one date, have a nice dinner and then say: 'That was nice – what are you doing in six weeks' time? I'm going to Chittagong'" – *South Africa captain* **Graeme Smith** *explains why love and cricket do not always go hand in hand*

"I'm crap at talking to girls. I really need them to come and chat to me, but I'm learning a lot from the England guys" – *England swing bowler* **Jimmy Anderson**, *before he married a former Miss UK*

"When I told my children I was retiring, they got a bit disappointed because they didn't think I was going to play backyard cricket with them. They said, 'Can you still play with us?' I said, 'I can'" – *Warne again*

"Warne managed to settle numerous scores in the construction of his list and the only surprise was his mother was not ranked a few places ahead of his former captain" – *Peter Roebuck after Warne ranks Steve Waugh – never his closest ally – at No. 26 in his list of 50 best cricketers*

"At first all I could think about was celebrating a Test wicket and then it sunk in and I wondered how Andrea was feeling at that moment" – *Mixed emotions for England's* **Craig White** *after dismissing Australia's Darren Lehmann, husband of White's sister, in a Test at Adelaide*

"Phil does it to me all the time but I, unfortunately, cannot go and whinge to Viv Richards" – *Frances Edmonds after Gordon Greenidge complains her husband Phil had been sledging him in the 1985-86 series*

"No matter what happens, a mother will always love her son" – **Penny Pietersen**, *mother of Kevin, after a haircut described by Ian Botham as looking like a dead mongoose*

"He might have women throwing themselves at him now, but that is only due to who he is – because he's not the best looking bloke, is he?" – *Kevin's brother, Bryan, adds to the humiliation*

"I know people say losing the semi-final is like kissing your sister, but we can take huge positives out of the World Cup" – *South Africa coach Mickey Arthur after defeat to Australia in 2007*

"He's definitely not a relative. In fact, I don't even know who he is. If I were his great-uncle than his grandfather would have to be my brother. I have a brother, Keith, but he doesn't have any kids" – *West Indian Sir Clyde Walcott denies the claim by the father of the Arsenal and England footballer Theo Walcott that Clyde and Theo are related*

"I've got a wife and child now and don't have much time to worry about toilet seats and taping bats to the ceiling" – *South Africa's Neil McKenzie claims he is over his obsessive-compulsive tendencies*

"Lynn believed the opener's job was to wear the shine off the new ball. He tried to do it by bouncing the ball off the roads outside the Oval" – *Neil Marks on his brother, the hard-hitting South Australian opener*

"We had one or two disagreements but once he realised he was wrong and I was right we moved on" – *Alan Butcher on working with his son Mark at Surrey*

"Physically sick but still watching" – *Nicola Fletcher, daughter of England coach Duncan, texts her mother Marina on the nerve-wracking final day of the Ashes in 2005*

"It was out of this world! I had a fantastic time with him. The best part was watching him on the pitch. He would look at me and wave. He said that having me there made him less lonely and homesick" – *Junita Bergman, mother of South Africa batsman JP Duminy, on accompanying her son on tour in Sydney in 2008-09*

"I think my mum has been telling me I'm the number one spinner for the last ten years so that's enough pressure for me" – *England off-spinner Graeme Swann*

"She tells me the same thing she always does, to back my ability, and it's the same thing Troy Cooley says to us every day" – *Australia seamer Nathan Bracken on the inspirational advice of his mother-in-law, Lenore Rich*

"I was waiting by the phone all the time and, to be honest, I would have been a prick to live with for those two weeks" – *Australia wicketkeeper Brad Haddin waits for the selectors to break the good news*

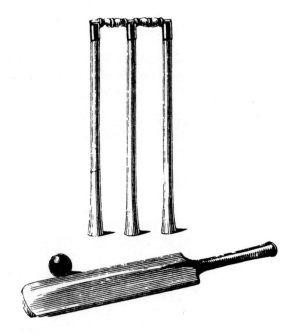

CHAPTER 16

COUNTY CRICKET

"I composed these lines when a summer wind/ Was blowing the elm leaves dry,/ And we were seventy-six for seven/ And they had CB Fry" – *John Betjeman's poem 'Cheltenham'*

"It's a lot more stable financially than football, a more pleasant environment; and the players are more humble and down-to-earth" – *Somerset chief executive Richard Gould, previously commercial director of Bristol City FC*

"I was brought up to believe that the finest county in England (not only in size) is Yorkshire; that cricket is the greatest game in the world; and that the cricketers who play it best come from Yorkshire" – *'A Country Vicar' from* The Happy Cricketer *by Frederick Muller, published in 1947*

"No writer of novels could make a picture of Yorkshire life half as full of meaning as the one drawn every year in matches between Lancashire and Yorkshire" – *Neville Cardus*

"We all meet on the first morning, say 'How do you do' and nowt else for three days, except 'How's that'" – *Yorkshire opener Roy Kilner on the Roses match*

"I'm glad to hear that at last Hampshire have come to their senses in making a Yorkshireman chairman" – *Yorkshire captain Brian Sellers congratulates Geoffrey Ford, born in Dewsbury, on his new job in 1956*

"A lotus land for batsman, a place where it was always afternoon and 360 for 2 wickets" – *Cardus on Trent Bridge*

"Essentially, The Oval is truer London than is Lord's. The Oval, as it were, is Dickens; Lord's is Thackeray" – *RC Robertson-Glasgow*

"The Test selectors' choice, anyway in earlier times, seems to have favoured Middlesex, Surrey, Yorkshire, Lancashire, Nottinghamshire, and Kent on the whole. Leicestershire was noted more for hunting, Northamptonshire for squires and spires" – *Robertson-Glasgow proves that the notion of fashionable and non-fashionable counties existed even in the early 1960s*

"I'm bowling this end. Which end do you want, Len?" – *Jack Flavell to his Worcestershire new-ball partner Len Coldwell*

"I absolutely insist that all my boys should be in bed before breakfast" – *Colin Ingleby-Mackenzie on the philosophy that helped his Hampshire side win their first county championship title in 1961*

"Yorkshire only ever booked a hotel for two nights when they came to Cardiff or Swansea" – *Glamorgan captain Wilf Wooller in the days when Yorkshire were expected to win the championship*

"That load of madmen will never win anything until they learn some self-discipline" – *Ray Illingworth on the Essex dressing room of the 1970s*

"You can't consider yourself a county cricketer until you've eaten half a ton of lettuce" – *West Indies all-rounder Garry Sobers, who spent seven seasons with Nottinghamshire*

"We've decided to change our name from Sussex to Macintosh, because we're always getting pissed on" – *Sussex captain Alan Wells in the days when his team weren't up to much*

"I had an extra pray and asked Allah to give us another championship. If you give 100 per cent then Allah will always favour you" – *Pakistan and Sussex leg-spinner Mushtaq Ahmed after Sussex celebrate their second title in 2006*

"I would like to thank Allah too because he's clearly played his part" – *Mushtaq's captain at Sussex, Chris Adams*

"In England, they have 18 counties and they call it first-class cricket and it's absolutely useless" – *Former South Africa and Hampshire batsman Barry Richards*

"During the depths of winter, the ghosts of cricketers long since dead no doubt will haunt Bramhall Lane, and from time to time if they listen carefully enough, football spectators may hear an occasional 'owzat' or 'gerra move on, Lancasheer'" – *Journalist Eric Todd on the last day of cricket in Sheffield*

"The biggest problem is that [the ECB] think the game is for members. It's not. It's for the whole country" – *Ian Botham*

"County cricket in its present form fulfils no useful purpose whatsoever. Very few people turn up to watch, it doesn't prepare people for a higher level of cricket and it doesn't attract television deals or sponsorship" – **Mike Atherton**

"Unless we change our domestic structure the England team will go on as it has for years. We will win some games and from time to time we nudge up a notch in the rankings but there will be no clear upward curve, which is what we need" – **Michael Vaughan**

"The big problem with Bob was that he wanted us all to be Test cricketers" – *One-cap wonder and future England selector James Whitaker on Bob Simpson's reign as coach of Leicestershire*

"Just fancy that!" – *Simpson's response*

"Those who run cricket in this country, especially at the domestic level, are for the most part a self-serving, pusillanimous and self-important bunch of myopic dinosaurs unable to take any but the shortest-term view of everything" – *Journalist and broadcaster Henry Blofeld offers his view of those in charge of English cricket, in 2003*

"Trusting county committee men to do what is best for the national game is like putting Brer Fox in charge of chickens" – Wisden *editor* **Scyld Berry**

"Without overseas players, the English county game would be dead" – *New Zealander Richard Hadlee in the mid-1980s*

"English cricket is like a sandwich. The English team is on top and the recreational game … is at the bottom, disenfranchised. In the middle, the soft filling, are the counties, like Northants, Leicestershire, Derbyshire, employing 450 full-time professionals and hiring all the Kolpaks and EU players they want" – *Former England fast bowler **Bob Willis***

"Ninety per cent of our members would rather see Northamptonshire win the county championship than see England win the Ashes" – *Northants chief executive **Steve Coverdale**, interviewed on Sky, neatly sums up the problems facing English cricket*

"The fans don't give a monkey's where their players are from. They just want to see their team winning" – ***Mark Tagg**, Coverdale's successor, after Northants stuffed their side with South Africans*

"Signing Kolpak players is like Internet shopping. Instead of getting out there and doing the hard yards trying to find what you're looking for, you can just have it delivered to your door" – ***Ashley Giles**, Warwickshire's director of cricket*

"No thanks, I can get three Kolpaks for that" – *County coach to an agent, who had asked for an £80,000 salary for his client*

"They're mostly businessmen in their late forties, not the old farts we're used to hearing about, and they know what they're doing" – ***Mike Soper**, previously a candidate for the role of ECB chairman, has a different view*

"We have a 19th-century ground, which we are required to bring into the 21st century of sportsground safety compliance … somehow the 20th century passed us by" – *Sussex chairman **David Green***

"If he'd had his way, we'd have stood up before the start of each match and belted out a couple of choruses of The Red Flag" – ***Ian Botham** on Geoff Cook's attempts to build a "socialist cricket republic" at Durham, devoid of a "star system"*

"The typical 1990s cricketer was a decent, regular middlebrow man who read the *Daily Mail* and Wilbur Smith novels and (except in Lancashire) dressed in C&A" – *Middlesex seamer **Simon Hughes***

"I might have done some dumb things in my time, but I think that is one of the dumbest things I have ever seen in my life. It was just absolutely ridiculous" – *Hampshire captain* **Shane Warne** *after Nottinghamshire pip his side to the championship in 2005 thanks to Kent's "dumb" decision to chase 420 against Notts*

"We're the new Surrey" – **Paul Collingwood** *after Durham get three players – him, Steve Harmison and Liam Plunkett – into the England team in 2005-06*

"The big difference this year is that it's been a bloody awful summer all over the country. I've been going to other counties and hearing them say how much rain they've had, and said, 'What a pity. We've been putting up with this for 100-odd years'" – *Lancashire's chairman* **Jack Simmons** *struggles to shed any tears for his opponents after the damp summer of 2007*

"It felt quite weird when we buried it, but it was exciting. I am glad that part of me will be at Sophia Gardens forever. That is my legacy to the club and it feels right" – *Glamorgan's* **Mike Powell** *has a rib buried at Sophia Gardens after it was removed following complications in surgery*

"There must be two Justin Langers in the world" – **Ricky Ponting** *can't believe that Justin Langer, never shy of a word or two himself, wants sledging stopped in county cricket*

"Maybe if I had bent down and kissed his backside I would still be at Lancashire" – **Stuart Law** *on the "certain individual" at Old Trafford who questioned his commitment*

"People sitting up there drinking their gin and tonic don't have to deal with it" – **Law** *takes a swipe at the Lancashire suits after the club fails to offer Dominic Cork a new contract*

"Fans tell me the family feeling's gone. I can only say good. It was a pretty dysfunctional family" – *Glamorgan chairman* **Paul Russell** *after a raft of staff changes*

"The pitch-liaison officers, we had a few of them down here yesterday for an interview, which was just a bit of a *Muppet Show*" – *Kent captain* **Robert Key** *after his side are beaten by Durham on a sporty pitch at the Riverside*

"I haven't seen him bowl. I was asleep when we played them" – *Durham's* **Steve Harmison** *reacts to the surprise Test call-up of Nottinghamshire's Darren Pattinson*

"I'll probably go to Starbucks and waste a few hours" – *Somerset's* **Ian Blackwell** *reveals how he plans to spend the day after a one-day game is washed out*

"Essex cricketers are always willing volunteers for all worthy causes, especially when there is gratuitous female nudity involved" – *An Essex spokesman explains why it wasn't too hard persuading Alastair Cook to take part in a charity photoshoot involving copious splashes of body paint*

"I can't lie. I haven't enjoyed it" – *Australian* **Steve Rixon** *leaves Surrey after two years as coach*

"If we hadn't dropped 43 catches in the Championship, we wouldn't be where we are. It's in our hands, we hope. Or out of it, as the case has been so far" – *Rixon's successor,* **Alan Butcher,** *has frustrations of his own in 2008. He was sacked at the end of the season*

"When I first joined Middlesex there was a big cards school when it rained … now, with all the public schoolboys in the Middlesex team, they play Scrabble" – **Mark Ramprakash**

"Fears that an escapee from the nearby Ford prison had melted into the crowd led to a strong police presence on the second day" – Wisden *report of the county championship match between Sussex and Yorkshire at Arundel in June 2002*

"You cannot even get a coffee for love or loose change" – *Journalist* **Will Buckley** *bemoans facilities at Essex's HQ in Chelmsford*

"We can confirm it is certainly possible to get a cup of coffee for 'loose change' – if not necessarily 'love'" – *An Essex spokesman hits back*

"Essex will be looking into it very seriously. If it is considered that our particular eagle has any Nazi connotations then we will remove it henceforth" – *The* **same spokesman** *after Barclays Bank was asked to dispense with its own eagle by its Dutch merger partner, ABN Amro*

PA ANNOUNCERS

"Ladies and gentlemen, a correction to your scorecards: for 'FJ Titmus' read 'Titmus FJ'" – *Announcer at Lord's reassures the crowd about the professional status of off-spinner Fred Titmus*

"Would the cigarette please sit down?" – *Announcer at The Oval after a man dressed as a cigarette to promote Surrey's smoking ban walks behind the bowler's arm*

"In view of Somerset's negative approach to this game, we are willing to refund the admission money of any spectator who wishes to call at the county office" – *Wilf Wooller, captain of Glamorgan turned secretary, surprises the Swansea crowd with an announcement on the loudspeaker*

"I am about to read the Glamorgan bowling figures and I suggest small boys or anyone of nervous disposition cover their ears" – *Glamorgan announcer Byron Denning after Worcestershire racked up a huge total at Abergavenny*

"News from the South" – *Announcer at Derby after local man Devon Malcolm is left out of England's squad to play Australia in the third Test in 1993*

"It is to be assumed that Mr Trevor Bailey was unavailable for selection" – *The Glamorgan announcer following the news that Nasser Hussain – one of several Essex players in the England side in 1993 – had been called up to the Test team*

TWENTY20

"It was more a means to an end than an end itself. It was your fun-size Mars bar, a little taste of cricket that hopefully would get people who merely tolerated cricket – rather than those who considered themselves fans of the game – to upgrade to one-day and maybe four- and five-day cricket" – *Stuart Robertson, the marketing man generally regarded to have given birth to Twenty20*

"We know not everyone will enjoy Twenty20 cricket and we accept this but we must capitalise on cricket's wider appeal" – *Tim Lamb, ECB chief executive when Twenty20 was introduced in 2003*

"A journey into the unknown" – *Sussex captain Chris Adams*

"This'll never catch on" – *Unconvinced hack in the Oval press box ahead of Surrey's inaugural Twenty20 game against Middlesex in 2003*

"No more substantial than a game of noughts and crosses on the beach" – The Cricketer *magazine passes judgment*

"Mate, I would have been a bloody full-time IPL man. Stuff doing the rest of that stuff. Why wear yourself out bowling to boring blokes on flat pitches when you can bowl four overs for IPL? I'm serious. If you didn't think that way you'd have to be a bloody idiot" – *Australia fast bowler Jeff Thomson wishes he hadn't retired in 1986*

"He actually sent me a text message this morning and said, 'I can't believe you're worth double what I am!'" – *Australia batsman, David Hussey, sold for $625,000 to IPL franchise Kolkata Knight Riders, enjoys hearing from his brother Mike, who fetched $350,000 from Chennai Super Kings*

"There was a little element of feeling like a cow" – *Australia wicketkeeper* Adam Gilchrist *on his emotions after the first IPL player auction*

"He is Moses of the game who has shown the path to blazing success" – *India all-rounder* **Ravi Shastri** *heaps praise on IPL commissioner and chairman Lalit Modi at the opening ceremony in April 2008*

"Six weeks' razzle-dazzle enough to consign over a hundred years of Test cricket to the dump? You must be off your rocker" – *David Gower*

"In almost 20 years of playing the game at the highest level, I don't think I've ever experienced the intensity and passion from a crowd like we had in the IPL, except for maybe the Ashes" – *Shane Warne, captain of the victorious Rajasthan Royals at the inaugural IPL*

"I've probably bowled the worst last over in Twenty20 history. Twenty20 is good for the game but not for the ego" – *Deccan Chargers' Andrew Symonds after his compatriot Warne hit him for 16 in three balls to win the match for Rajasthan*

"All the organisers are doing by making scantily-clad white women dance in front of huge crowds is to stoke the base voyeuristic and sexual insecurities of the Indian male. It is revolting, appalling and shows the game in very poor light" – *Historian* **Ramachandra Guha** *on the IPL cheerleaders*

"The girls in skimpy dresses should be removed from the ground as this is distracting the batsman" – *Who is* **Shahid Afridi**, *Deccan Chargers' Pakistan all-rounder, trying to kid?*

"My team told me that they have yet to meet a better human being than me. This is a huge compliment" – *Kolkata Knight Riders franchise owner* **Shah Rukh Khan** *doesn't have time for false modesty*

"I am as dedicated to my Knights as I am to my kids" – *Shah Rukh gushes once more*

"This is not cricket. This is the greatest divide between the rich and the poor. With that kind of money, you could have built another cement factory" – *Jaswant Singh, leader of the Opposition, criticises the IPL in the Indian Parliament*

"The IPL was only four overs a game and it was like a paid holiday; you only had to work hard if you felt like it, which is probably why we finished second-last" – *South Africa fast bowler* **Dale Steyn** *following his stint with Bangalore Royal Challengers. He later apologised*

"Look, Twenty20 is such a fast game that you have to remain focused all the time. We don't even have enough time for sledging" – *David Hussey*

"I think the pace of the game will help as there will be no time to sledge. Well, maybe a little sneaky one here or there" – **Warne** *clarifies the matter*

"I'm not too sure whether I would have been bought at the auction anyway" – **Michael Vaughan** *explains why he pulled out of the player auction for the 2009 IPL*

"The best part was in the bar afterwards. Everybody was banned so it was a pretty relaxed atmosphere. I had a blast" – *New Zealand's* **Shane Bond** *on life in the so-called rebel Indian Cricket League*

"If we can have BMW and Mercedes as separate companies why can't we have both IPL and ICL?" – *Aggrieved ICL frontman* **Kapil Dev**

"When you go to your grave, people will remember what you did with your life rather than how much money you made" – *Australia opener* **Justin Langer** *explains why he opted out of the IPL*

"In terms of sporting endeavour and prestige, the IPL is to cricket what diarrhoea is to dodgy curry houses – an unfortunate by-product" – *New Zealand journalist* **Paul Lewis**

"Test cricket may be compared to the finest Scotch, 50-overs a side to Indian Made Foreign Liquor, and 20-20 to the local hooch" – *Ramachandra Guha*

"I haven't seen it. I am a bit of a purist; a bit of a snob. I like to see technique. I like to see the aesthetic beauty of the game" – *England fast bowler* **Frank Tyson** *on Twenty20*

"I don't even bother with it, it's rubbish" – *Tyson's former team-mate* **Fred Trueman** *on the same subject*

"Youngsters need to learn good techniques ... they cannot do that by watching rubbish. There is nothing good about Twenty20 cricket. People who disagree don't know what they are talking about" – *West Indies fast bowler* **Michael Holding**

"Twenty20 is a joke. I wouldn't have enjoyed playing it at all" – *Australia batsman* **Doug Walters** *joins the chorus*

"I might. But not if I am going to miss *The Bold and The Beautiful*" – *Australia opener* **Arthur Morris** *when asked if he'll be watching the All-Stars v Australian XI Twenty20 match*

"If one-day cricket was pyjama cricket, then Twenty20 is underwear cricket" – *India batsman* **Navjot Sidhu**

"This cricket is like a burger, you can have it once a week but for a whole meal, you need to return to Test cricket. More than once a week, and it will give you a tummy ache" – **Sidhu** *tries another tack...*

"Test cricket is like classical music which has survived since ancient ages. One-dayers are like film music that leaves people enthralled and Twenty20 cricket is like disco and rap which provides occasional pleasure in short bursts" – *... and another*

"It's like three-minute Maggi noodles. Bang, bang, and it is over. For me, it is not cricket" – *Sri Lanka captain* **Arjuna Ranatunga** *on the IPL*

"Twenty20 is not cricket. It's pure entertainment. VVS Laxman and Rahul Dravid batting out a whole day against the Australians – now that is cricket" – *Author* **Jeffrey Archer** *speaking during the IPL in 2008*

"Twenty20 cricket is lovely. Three hours and done and dusted" – *South Africa all-rounder* **Lance Klusener**

"Cricket will make a great deal of money in the short term, money it has no obvious need for and will mostly waste, and it will be left a coarser, crueller, crasser game as a result" – *Journalist and historian* **Gideon Haigh** *on the spread of Twenty20*

"People pay their money but some feel it gives them the right to shout abuse to different players. Perhaps that is a bit of football mentality coming in and as a player that is not particularly nice" – *Surrey's* **Mark Ramprakash** *on the fans attracted by Twenty20*

"People have many different motivations. For some it's ego, some it's for appearances, some it's for cash, for some it's to be a pain in the arse and for some it's to get out of the house" – *Australia leg-spinner* **Stuart MacGill** *reacts to news that 47 per cent of contracted Australian players would consider quitting international cricket to cash in on Twenty20 money in India*

"The game's called Twenty20, it's not called One1" – *New Zealand captain* **Daniel Vettori** *after being hit for 25 in cricket's first Super Over by West Indies' Chris Gayle. The scores had originally finished all square after 20 overs*

"Twenty20 is here to stay, as is the future of coloured-clothes cricket, but white clothes separate the men from the boys" – **Kevin Pietersen** *lays out his priorities*

"People who abuse us are not going to pay for my children's school fees in 15 years' time, are they?" – **Pietersen** *reacts to criticism of playing Twenty20 cricket for money*

"I find it boring, but I'm not a purist" – **Sir Allen Stanford** *on Test cricket*

"Twenty20 has the potential to be the most popular team sport in the whole world in maybe less than ten years" – **Stanford's** *vision*

"This is a bizarre concept. I find it a strange one. I don't know quite what to make of it but I'm sure I could put the money to a good home if we win" – *Andrew Flintoff tries to contain himself at the prospect of winning $1m of Stanford's money*

"I am the world's worst person with money. If I got £360,000 after tax, I would probably buy a bright pink Ferrari and waste it all like a stupid Premiership footballer" – *Tongue placed firmly in cheek,* **Graeme Swann** *on what he'd do with the profits*

"I'd buy Luton Town football club" – **Monty Panesar**, *resident of Luton*

"The players know there won't be any open-top bus parades if we beat a Stanford team" – *Pietersen dampens down expectations in advance*

"Who doesn't want a million? You got to be crazy!" – *Gayle, captain of the Stanford Superstars, can't understand the moral equivocation about winning all that money for three hours' work*

"KP already has plenty of money so he should make it easy for us" – *Gayle to Pietersen, captain of the England XI*

"Maybe some of these guys are thinking about their bank accounts before they start playing" – *Viv Richards watches one fielder after another drop a catch during the Stanford Super Series against a backdrop of poor-quality floodlights*

"When this was announced in June I was a hero; now I'm a skunk in October" – *Stanford reflects on the negative press attracted by his money-spinning Super Series*

"The longer this week goes on and the more people make of it, the more you just want to get it over with really" – *Pietersen feels the vibes*

"Anderson mugged on way to the bank" – *Headline in the* **Independent** *after ever-present England seamer James Anderson is dropped for the Stanford match*

"There were a few gobsmacked faces. I did not see it because I was bowling at the time but I think Matt Prior had a look of shock on his face" – *England seamer* **Stuart Broad** *after Prior's pregnant wife, Emily, was seen on the giant screen bouncing on Stanford's knee*

"English cricket has become Stanford's WAG" – **Mike Atherton**

"People say he walks around like he owns the place. Well, he does" – **Graeme Swann** *on Stanford*

"There never has been, and there never will be, an easy way to make money. It requires discipline, knowledge, experience, hard work and plain common sense" – *Advice from Stanford, a wealth investor, to clients in a newsletter. Stanford was accused of $8bn-worth of fraud in February 2009*

"Stanford was a sleazebag. I was very uncomfortable with the whole Stanford thing" – **Pietersen**, *who nevertheless signed up to become a Stanford 'ambassador'*

"Incompetence at a spectacular level" – *Hampshire chairman* **Rod Bransgrove's** *view on the accusation that the ECB failed to conduct proper due diligence on Stanford*

"My Blackberry has broken down and I've had over 9,000 emails saying, 'Don't pay attention'" – *ECB chairman* **Giles Clarke** *reveals the support he had since Stanford was accused of fraud*

"The letters ECB stand for the England and Wales Cricket Board not the European Central Bank" – *Somerset chairman* **Andy Nash** *defends the ECB's failure to uncover proof of financial wrongdoing by Stanford*

"Are you this guy?" – **FBI agent** *to Stanford, spotted in a car in Fredericksburg, south-west of Virginia, having disappeared for two days after being accused of fraud*

"Considering that we invented Twenty20, India should not have got there first. It is important that we act quickly" – **Sean Morris**, *chief executive of the Professional Cricketers' Association, urges the English game to respond to the IPL*

CRICKETERS AND MONEY

"He did not spend twopence during the tour" – *An Australian team-mate of* **Don Bradman** *after the 1930 Ashes trip*

"I had started up a business selling Christmas cards and I could make more money in a week in Scotland than I could playing for England" – **Ray Illingworth** *explains why he once turned down a tour of Pakistan, as recounted by Dermot Reeve*

"I can't forget the time he once told a team meeting: 'The day I stop thinking of money, I will stagnate'" – **Bishan Bedi** *on his former Indian team-mate Sunil Gavaskar*

"[He asked] why I would want to waste money on an expensive restaurant when you could get perfectly adequate food for a quarter of the price in a cheap restaurant. It was a small example, but it was the moment I knew something had gone very wrong and it disturbed me. I couldn't get the idea out of my head he would rather eat a burger than have a very pleasant meal" – **Gary Kirsten** *on how his team-mate Hansie Cronje's eating habits proved telling*

"In a moment of stupidity and weakness I allowed Satan and the world to dictate terms to me. The moment I took my eyes off Jesus my whole world turned dark" – **Cronje**

"I am not addicted to alcohol or nicotine, but I believe this is very similar to an alcohol problem" – **Cronje** *on his 'unfortunate love of money'*

"I'd bat like that too if I had your money" – *Yorkshire wicketkeeper* **David Bairstow** *to Matthew Fleming after Fleming hit the first two balls of his debut game for Kent for six*

"At the crease he looks a million dollars, which is probably what he has got tucked away somewhere" – *Surrey captain* **Mark Butcher** *on former cricketer, now author, Ed Smith*

CRICKETERS AND MONEY

"One thing that I do find unattractive is when people who are making money out of the game criticise those of us who are volunteers" – *ECB chairman* **Giles Clarke** *hits out*

"We have been around for more than 220 years. We've outlived world wars and revolutions, let alone the odd financial crisis" – **Keith Bradshaw**, *chief executive of MCC, plays down concerns over the credit crunch*

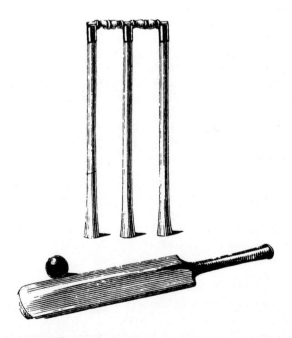

FROM THE SUBLIME...

"I do love cricket – it's so very English" – *French actress **Sarah Bernhardt** … while watching a game of football*

"Look here, Neville, I've got an idea. What about me slipping a carbon paper into my copy today for you and you can do the same for me tomorrow. We both write the same sort of stuff" – *Straight-talking (and -writing) Australian **Sid Barnes** to flowery Englishman Neville Cardus*

"What they failed to say was that six of them long-hops were *straight* long-hops" – *Middlesex leg-spinner **Jim Sims**, reacts to the* Evening Standard *headline "Sims takes eight wickets with long-hops"*

"Every television in the Ballistic Early Warning System room was tuned to Lord's. The Russians could have taken us out at any time" – *A civil servant tells Professor Peter Hennessey about Britain's vulnerability as the 1963 Lord's Test against West Indies approached its gripping finale*

"This is rather fun, old chap, is it not?"
"I've been in funnier situations than this, ya Pommie bastard"
"I beg your pardon"
"I'm sorry, it's just something I've picked up from the locals" – *Conversation between **Colin Cowdrey** and **David Lloyd** as England face Lillee and Thomson on a Perth flyer in 1974-75*

"The injury did, in fact, confirm my earlier statement about 'Thommo' that I could play him with my c*ck" – *Lloyd after having his box turned inside out by Thomson in the same game*

"In a flat high above Karachi, an 18-year-old kid strung out on heroin danced cheerfully around the room in front of me pointing to his erection, which he referred to as his Imran Khan, the name of the handsome Pakistan cricket captain" – *The novelist **Hanif Kureishi** on his first visit to his native city*

"It included the exposure of parts of the human anatomy not usually seen on the cricket field, the pulling of faces and the mimicking of various bowlers' actions" – ***David Boon** on Ian Botham's final over in first-class cricket, for Durham v Australia in 1993*

"The Indians used to call him 'Iron Bottom', but he wasn't – not after all that f**kin' curry" – ***John Emburey** on Botham's travails on the subcontinent*

"He basically just grabbed me by the hand [and walked me] into the toilets and was threatening me to put suppositories up his backside" – ***Mike Hussey** reveals how Tom Moody made him feel part of the Western Australia dressing-room*

"Take a good look at this arse of mine, you'll see plenty of it this summer" – *England's **David Steele** to Australia's wicketkeeper Rodney Marsh in 1975. Steele ended up averaging 60 in the series*

"It gets you down a little bit if people think it's more entertaining to run on the pitch with no clothes on" – *England captain **Nasser Hussain** after the Old Trafford Test against West Indies in 2000 is interrupted by four streakers*

"By the time a wicket fell I was desperate. I turned towards some trees and answered the call of nature. Hardly anyone saw" – ***Wayne Radcliffe**, a cricketer for Newmillerdam, is banned for five years by the Wakefield and District Cricket Union, for peeing on the pitch while fielding in the covers in 1995*

"A dry fart" – *England spinner **Phil Edmonds** responds to a reporter who asked him what he was most looking forward to on a return from India*

"Compton, D. C. S c White b Cheese, the *Bristol Evening Post* later announced" – *Comedian **John Cleese**, playing for Clifton College, after supposedly dismissing Denis Compton twice in one innings*

"I was a bit concerned my name wasn't going to fit on the shirt" – *England women's all-rounder Ebony-Jewel Cora-Lee Camellia Rosamond Rainford-Brent*

"Craig McDermott must surely know by now, you can't be bowling there to Carlisle Best" – *West Indies batsman Carlisle Best commentates on his own strokeplay, as related by Australia's short leg David Boon*

"As captain I spoke to all the players, informing them that we would be going to the Wankhede stadium to practise, as arranged. Graeme Fowler, never one to miss a good line, said: 'What? Target practice?'" – *David Gower on the tour of India in 1984, when Prime Minister Indira Gandhi and the British High Commissioner were both assassinated*

"I'm not going to be Adolf Warne or anything like that" – *Shane Warne reacts to reports he is seeking German citizenship on account of his mother, Brigitte*

"For the next few minutes I was gasping for breath under water" – *Bob Woolmer after suggesting to Geoff Boycott, sharing a bath after a game for MCC, that Kent's players felt he had a weakness down the leg-side*

"The Jaguar driver came over and said it was dangerous playing cricket so near a main road. It was pointed out to him that they had been playing here since 1774" – *Jim Smith, the chairman of Aldwick CC in Sussex, after a six bounced off the top of a bus and dented a Jag*

"You won't get around there, China" – *Pat Symcox to Shane Warne, the ball before Warne bowls him round his legs in a Test at Sydney*

"I knew that Daryll was a bit fragile at times, but never imagined he would go to a shrink to learn how to read the googly" – *Warne on his buddy, Daryll Cullinan of South Africa*

"At one stage I had to sit in with a lawyer and prove I could understand English. Seriously, mate. He sat there and said, 'I'm a bit embarrassed about this, but I need to know you understand English and can speak it properly.' I said, 'You are joking'. So he asked me where I was born and I said 'Brisbane'. He seemed happy that I understood the question" – *Fair-dinkum Aussie Stuart Law on his fight for British citizenship*

"It would be worth getting a pair just to walk out against the Aussies and hear what they had to say" – *Law in mischievous, post-qualified mood*

"Absent, babysitting" – *Scorebook entry for a player named Cordingly in a game between Cliffe and Yalding in Kent, June 1996*

"Ramprakash, after dislocating his toe on the pavilion steps fetching a cup of tea, batted at No. 7 and scored 11" – Wisden Almanack 2006

"I can hit a golf ball a long way but for some reason I struggle to hit a cricket ball a long way" – *England opener* **Alastair Cook**

"*Test Match Special* is all chocolate cakes and jolly japes, but I didn't enjoy being called a wheelie-bin, and nor did my family" – **Ashley Giles** *is not amused by Henry Blofeld's on-air description of his approach to the crease*

"He may not quite have made the leap to Hedley Verity status but he has certainly left wheelie-binnery far behind" – **Blofeld** *apologises*

"Yovich bowled the first ball after the break with a red apple, an event recorded on the official scoresheet" – **Wisden** *report on a game between Northern Districts and Wellington in New Zealand*

"I have to watch my skin more and make sure that I look good and have had my hair done. I could easily lose my crown back to David Beckham if I'm not careful" – **Andrew Flintoff** *on the pressures of being a gay icon*

"That means I can drive a flock of sheep through the town centre, drink for free in no less than 64 pubs, and get a lift home with a policeman when I become inebriated. What more could you want?" – *Flintoff is awarded the freedom of the city of Preston after the 2005 Ashes*

"We did not lose this Test because of jelly beans" – *England captain* **Michael Vaughan** *at Trent Bridge in 2007 after India's Zaheer Khan had reacted angrily to the sight of sweets at the crease as he came out to bat*

"They should be forced to play their next game in short trousers" – *Journalist* **John Woodcock** *begs to differ*

"He went into the club and was shown an inappropriate area" – *ECB spokesman on **Paul Collingwood**'s ill-advised trip to a strip club in South Africa*

"Well, thank God we've arrived in Sri Lanka, where there don't appear to be any strip clubs whatsoever" – *Collingwood breathes a sigh of relief*

"One day I was up on the roof, the next I was playing at the MCG. Now I'm never going near a roof again" – *Nottinghamshire and Victoria seamer **Darren Pattinson** shelves plans to resume his career as a roof tiler after taking six wickets against Lancashire. Two months later he was picked for England*

"Who writes these headlines?" – *Vaughan to John Etheridge, cricket correspondent of the* Sun, *after his newspaper had described the "shellshocked" England captain as "Vaughan the prawn" (geddit?)*

"I'm never, ever, going to succumb to the Playstation" – *Nasser Hussain reveals the kind of single-mindedness that has helped him score 5,430 Test runs*

"On the upside, I've always got a decent stockpile of miniature toiletries" – *England and Essex all-rounder **Ronnie Irani** on one of the perks of travel*

"Before the game we said, 'Let's make history today.' Well, we made history" – *Luuk van Troost, captain of the Netherlands, after South Africa's Herschelle Gibbs's hits Dutch leg-spinner Daan van Bunge for six sixes in an over at the 2007 World Cup*

"What a stupid question: 'When was the last time you had a row with your partner?'" – *Australia's **Andrew Symonds**, reading out loud a question in a magazine to his team-mates, confuses a boating trip with a domestic argument*

"Is that it?" – *Businessman spies the Ashes urn for the first time on show in the South Australian Museum in Adelaide in 2006-07*

"Gunther is a guy who lives in the mountains and doesn't get enough oxygen to the brain and that makes him crazy. As soon as I get thrown the ball, it's like a little switch goes in my head. Gunther takes over" – *South Africa seamer **Andre Nel** ascribes his on-field behaviour to someone else altogether*

"Nobody understands cricket. To understand cricket you gotta know what a crumpet is" – *Raphael, one of the Teenage Mutant Ninja Turtles, after being assaulted with a cricket bat*

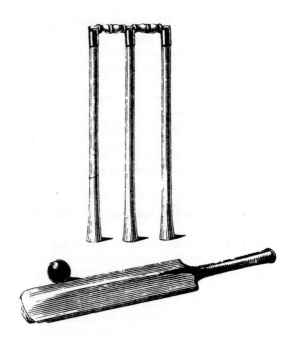

CHAPTER 19

APOCRYPHA?

"I declare" – *WG Grace, as a fielder is about to catch him*

"They have come to watch me bat, not you bowl" – *WG replaces the bails after being bowled by the first delivery of an exhibition match*

"The old man cheat? No sir! He was too clever for that" – *Gloucestershire player to writer and critic **Neville Cardus** on the perennially thorny subject of WG*

"We'll get 'em in singles" – *George Hirst's supposed rejoinder to Wilfred Rhodes at The Oval in 1902 with England, nine down, needing 15 to beat Australia*

"There'd have been just as much sense if he'd said: 'We'll get 'em in sixes'" – *Rhodes dismisses the quote*

"Committee has decided that there are to be no lbw decisions in this match"
"And if middle stump is knocked out, it's just a nasty accident, eh?" – *Supposed conversation before a Gents v Players match at Blackpool between a **committee man** and Nottinghamshire batsman **George Gunn***

"In my day we would have put our front foot down the pitch and hit him back over his head. We would have charged him like the Light Brigade! Why didn't you charge Rorke, Cowdrey?"
"I couldn't, sir. If I had stepped forward to drive, Rorke would have stepped on my toe…" – *England batsman **Colin Cowdrey** in conversation with an MCC member on the perils of facing Australia's 6ft 5in giant Gordon Rorke*

"What a performance. I'd give anything to meet that Laker" – *Random **punter** to England off-spinner Jim Laker in a pub after he had taken 19 wickets at Old Trafford in 1956*

"Though the joke has persisted down the decades, there is no record that the famous scatological scorecard entry, Crapp c Hole b Ring, ever occurred" – **Wisden** *obituary of Australia leg-spinner Doug Ring*

"What if it had hit you an inch lower?"
"He'd have been caught in t'gully!" – *Brian Close, fielding at short leg, after a pull shot rebounded off his unprotected forehead and was caught at second slip (other versions have different combinations of field placings)*

"I'll get in t'road and you can catch t'rebound" – *Close to David Steele, at backward short leg, as West Indies defended against Derek Underwood and Pat Pocock at Lord's in 1976*

"Put your pads on and fight for Pakistan"
"But manager, I have already batted!"
"Never mind. Do as I say, for the honour of our country!" – *Reputed exchange between a* **Pakistan tour manager** *and an* **unnamed batsman** *during a collapse in a Test in England*

"You don't get a runner for being an overweight, unfit, fat c**t" – *Australia wicketkeeper* **Ian Healy** *to Sri Lanka captain Arjuna Ranatunga*

"Put a Mars bar on a length. That should do it" – *Healy's cunning plan to lure Ranatunga out of his crease*

"Then I'm sure Boony will get it before me" – *Ranatunga on Australia's equally barrel-chested short-leg fielder David Boon*

"You guys are f**king dead. All you guys are f**king history" – *England fast bowler* **Devon Malcolm** *after being hit on the head by South Africa's Fanie de Villiers at The Oval in 1994. Malcolm went on to take 9 for 57*

"What does it feel like to drop the World Cup?" – *Australia's* **Steve Waugh** *to South Africa's Herschelle Gibbs after Gibbs had dropped him at Headingley in 1999*

"I drive a Porsche, what car do you drive?" – *England wicketkeeper* **Matt Prior**'s *supposed taunt to Sachin Tendulkar at Trent Bridge in 2007*

"That Porsche comment ... why would I say that to Tendulkar? He's got aeroplanes" – *Prior tries to explain*

"I want us to rise from the ashes like a pheasant"
"I think you mean a phoenix"
"Shut up Strauss. I knew it was a bird beginning with F" – *One of Kevin Pietersen's first team-talks as England captain is interrupted by* **Andrew Strauss**

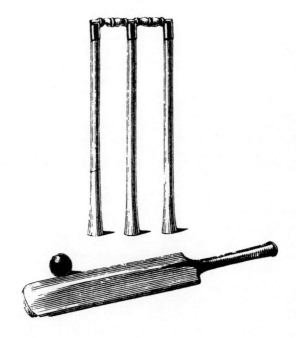

CHAPTER 20

AND FINALLY...

"Plus or minus twenty, shall we say?" – *One of the scorers at the end of AEJ Collins's 628 not out in a house match at Clifton College, Bristol, in 1899*

"Mr Compton, you very good player but the game must stop" – *Rioter to Denis Compton, playing for East Zone in India against the Australian Services*

"We were extremely careful not to become metric martyrs, so we complied with the written wishes of Westminster Council, and sold our turf in metric, rather than imperial measurements" – *Ted Dexter, president of the MCC, points out that the Lord's turf was not being sold for £10 per square foot*

"It's hard to explain an instant rapport between a visiting international cricket team and a local amateur brass band. But that's what it was" – *Australia captain Allan Border remembers the affection the 1985 Australian tourists felt for Headingley's Hammond Sauce Works band*

"I still have the butterflies but now they are flying in formation" – *Australia captain Mark Taylor after ending his barren spell in 1997 with a century at Edgbaston*

"If Rembrandt can do it, why can't I?" – *England wicketkeeper Jack Russell explains the thought process that persuaded him to take up painting*

"It's taught me that when I go on tour I have to take two alarm clocks" – *England spinner Graeme Swann learns his lesson after missing the team bus on tour in South Africa in 1999-2000*

"Ask me that again next month, when you're all in Dhaka and I'm in Rome, watching Chelsea playing Lazio!" – *Alec Stewart, asked if he regretted announcing his retirement*

"It's like playing football with your mate in the park and then watching him on TV at the World Cup and he's nutmegging Ronaldo" – *Ian Whitehead, a club cricketer for Burnley, where Jimmy Anderson was playing for the Third Eleven just months before destroying Pakistan in the 2003 World Cup*

"We are of the opinion that it was unethical for Gilchrist to use a squash ball to give an unfair advantage" – *Kangadaran Mathivanan, the secretary of the Sri Lankan cricket board, objects to the squash ball Adam Gilchrist put in his left glove to help with his grip during his match-winning 149 in the 2003 World Cup final*

"Fred could take three of the Aussies down, Steve Harmison would get stuck into two, I could take one ... but they've got some big guys in their squad" – *Andrew Strauss rates England's chances in a fist fight with the old enemy*

"It was a bit strange walking out to the middle with no players out there" – *Ian Bell, one of the not-out England batsmen as Pakistan refused to take the field after tea on the fourth day of the abandoned Oval Test in 2006*

"Who would you like to win, if you had to stick your neck out?" – *Moments before the prize raffle is drawn at the annual Professional Cricketers' Association dinner, impressionist Rory Bremner chats to hunched former fast bowler Gladstone Small*

"He deserved it. I love him. To see that cynical little man laughing again is just great" – *Kevin Pietersen spreads the love after Steve Harmison falls one short of a maiden Test fifty*

"One positive coming from that game was I could hear all this yelling and screaming coming from the background and it was Jason on the boundary" – *Ricky Ponting on the eagerness of Australia off-spinner Jason Krejza*

"He walked up the wicket and said 'I was thinking about doing that in bed last night', so the visualisation was there" – *Paul Collingwood reveals what Kevin Pietersen said after switch-hitting two sixes against New Zealand at Chester-le-Street in 2008*

"Grant's hit that high to long-off… It's coming this wayyyyyyyyyy… [sound of smashed glass]" – *BBC Wales commentator **Eddie Bevan** takes evasive action during a Twenty20 match at Cardiff*

"I don't know what that's all about, mate. The only person I can remember doing it was a wrestler called the Rock" – *Australia seamer **Jason Gillespie** on cricketers' increasing tendency to refer to themselves in the third person*

CRICKET AND ANIMALS

"What as, Charles? Trainer, jockey or horse?" – *Author **Denzil Batchelor** after CB Fry, already over 70, informed him he wanted to become involved in racing*

"Tell me, Mr Yardley, what kind of creatures are these Australian cricketers? No wonder England can't win" – *An old lady writes a letter to Norman Yardley after hearing on the radio that Ray Lindwall had two long legs, a short leg and a square leg*

"Merv Hughes" – *Hughes's Australian colleague **Steve Waugh** answers the question: "What is your favourite animal?"*

"Information in this game travels and people remember when someone is carrying on like a goose" – *Australia's **Andrew Symonds** on India fast bowler Sreesanth*

"We ran the bulls down in an old Landcruiser with the tyres on the front. We knocked them over and tied them up and whacked them in the back of what we call a lion cage and carted them off to the markets. It was great fun" – *Symonds on one of his favourite pastimes*

"I appreciate how wild pigs feel when they get caught in a spotlight out in the paddocks – there aren't too many places to hide once you are in the crosshairs" – *Symonds on the emotional fallout of the controversial Sydney Test in January 2008, when he claimed India's Harbhajan Singh called him a monkey*

CRICKET AND ANIMALS

"I'm always up for a challenge, but eating a kangaroo's bits is no way to prove yourself" – *England and Yorkshire seamer* **Darren Gough** *rules out an appearance on ITV's* I'm A Celebrity, Get Me Out Of Here…

"I feel so bad about mine, I'm going to tie it round my cat. It doesn't mean anything anymore. It's a joke" – *Geoff Boycott after England's players were awarded MBEs for beating Australia in 2005*

"Two hungry dogs, if you can use the metaphor, that circle each other in a ring… I as a spectator want to see that ability to gnash teeth" – *Australia opener* **Matthew Hayden** *on the dynamic of matches against India*

"It's just like if you let a dog roam on the streets eventually they become fearless, you know? That is how I feel right now" – *England all-rounder* **Ravi Bopara**, *speaking in 2008, is eager for a Test recall*

INDEX